The Best-Ever Web Sites
for the Topics You Teach

By Roberta Salvador

SCHOLASTIC
PROFESSIONAL BOOKS

New York • Toronto • London • Auckland • Sydney
Mexico City • New Delhi • Hong Kong

This book is lovingly dedicated
to my most wonderful teacher, P. C. Brahmachari,
and to my family.

Copyright © 2000 by Roberta Salvador

Cover design by Norma Ortiz
Interior design by Drew Hires
Interior illustrations by Drew Hires
Cover screenshots from Nasa's Jet Propulsion Laboratory (designed by Jayne Dutra), Ocean Planet/Smithsonian (designed by Gene Carl Feldman), and Scholastic.com.

ISBN 0-439-13115-4

Table of Contents

Introduction

The Internet is a powerful, almost limitless, resource for teachers and students. You can use it find up-to-the-minute background information to spice up your lessons, participate in online staff development, or communicate with experts to find a new way to teach a math concept. Your students can use it to ask experts questions, view video clips, and talk to other students. The Internet can, however, be overwhelming at times. With this resource, I hope to save you time by giving you addresses and descriptions of some of the best sites the Web has to offer. The high-quality sites are meant to complement the topics and concepts you teach so your time online is well-spent.

Internet Safety

Your students already understand the power of the Internet, but they may not always know whether the information they find is accurate or if it comes from a reputable source. That's where you enter the picture. Many schools have chosen to install "Internet filters," which block out certain Web sites based on specific words or phrases. More commonly, schools make the students (and their parents) responsible for "netiquette," or respectful behavior when using these powerful tools. You may want to have students and/or their parents or guardians sign a "responsible use contract," in which students are allowed to send and receive e-mail and to visit sites on the Web, provided this is done within sensible guidelines. Among other things, a responsible use contract asks students to pledge that they will not tamper with or trespass into another person's files, folders, e-mail, or passwords; will not visit inappropriate

Web sites; and will use the school's computer facilities in a responsible manner. A good example of school Internet and technology policies can be found on the Web site of the Bellingham, Washington, public schools (http://www.bham.wednet.edu /policies.htm). A reproducible Parent Internet Permission Form can be found there.

But even filters cannot discriminate as to whether information is of good quality or based on sloppy research, and again, here is where the teacher, librarian, or parent is indispensable as a Web mentor. Always encourage students to think critically about the source of the information they find.

Internet Address Changes

I've tried to choose sites for this book that I feel are well-established and have staying power. However, Internet sites sometimes change addresses or even close down, and you may occasionally find that you can no longer access one of the addresses we've listed in this book. It is always a good idea to check each site before having students visit it.

Finally, it is my hope that educators everywhere will explore the sites described in this book and sample the useful things they offer, to help nurture your students' love of knowledge, and to augment your own.

Quick Glossary of Terms

Bandwidth The volume of data that can be handled by a networked connection. A high amount of bandwidth is desirable because it enables the user to get more data at faster rates, allowing for smoother play of video and other media over the Web. (Imagine a garden hose carrying water; now imagine a fire hose shooting a stream. The latter represents the larger volume of data transfer that higher bandwidth provides.)

Browser (also called Web browser) A software program that allows users to view pages created in HTML (see definition below) on the Web, and "navigate" from one area to another (and one site to another) by pointing and clicking on-screen pictures, symbols, or "hot" text. The most widely used browsers today are Netscape Navigator and Microsoft Internet Explorer.

Bug A flaw in the software or hardware that prevents it from functioning properly.

CD-ROM Short for Compact Disc Read-Only Memory. One CD-ROM disc holds approximately 640 bytes of data, which makes it a great medium for multimedia—texts illustrated with images and music—or storing large amounts of text (e.g., reference books or encyclopedias).

Download When a "local" computer (your school or home PC) receives, via network transfer, a file or Web page from a "remote" computer or server. For example, a teacher who wishes to have a copy of the school calendar on his or her PC can log on to the district Web site and download a copy of the calendar to keep on file. To upload is to transfer a file from a "local" computer to a "remote" computer or server.

Home Page The main entry point, or "first page," to every Web site. Usually, the home page of a Web site will contain information on how to transfer to other parts of the site, or to related sites

HTML Short for Hypertext Markup Language. A standard computer coding language that allows the creation and viewing of pages on the Web. HTML works with Web browsers, which "understand" the code and set the arrangement of text and images on a Web page. (For example, breaking text to form a new paragraph, placing an image in a particular spot, or setting a background color. All of these commands are written in HTML.)

HTTP Abbreviation for Hypertext Transfer Protocol. It is used to access HTML pages on the World Wide Web. It begins most URLs (Web addresses), such as http://www.scholastic.com.

Internet The name for the globally interconnected networks that allow computers to communicate with one another. The Internet is supported by "backbone networks" of high-speed data lines connecting major information "hubs" (host systems that act as traffic managers) to one another so that messages can get to their correct recipients.

Modem A telecommunications device that links two computers together via a common phone or cable line. (The latter uses a portion of the cable that brings cable television to homes and schools, and is called a "cable modem.")

Multimedia An information presentation (such as a software program or Web site) that integrates text with various combinations of pictures, sound, and/or moving images, thereby incorporating multiple forms of media.

Network A group of computers connected to one another.

Server A computer that acts as an information hub, sharing information with other computers on the same network. For example, a software program that is shared by all computers in a network is usually installed on the server.

URL Uniform Resource Locator. This is the "Web address" that a user types into the address bar or window to call up a Web page onto his or her screen. (For NASA, the URL is http://www.nasa.gov.)

World Wide Web ("WWW") The mass of hyperlinked HTML-based documents that can be accessed from Web servers anywhere in the world.

Part

1

Science

▶ GENERAL RESOURCES

National Science Standards

http://www.nap.edu/readingroom/books/nses/html/6a.html

View the full National Science Education Standards with charts, graphs, and examples at this site.

The Science Explorer

http://www.exploratorium.edu/science_explorer/index.html

A wonderful online book of science projects, with step-by-step instructions students in the late primary and middle school grades can easily follow. Projects use everyday, simple materials: a geodesic dome built from gumdrops and toothpicks; a miniature "lava lite" made from oil, salt, and food coloring; and other creations that demonstrate various scientific principles. This site is just one part of the remarkable online branch of The Exploratorium, the famous children's museum. Check out all it has to offer at http://www.exploratorium.edu.

The Why Files

http://whyfiles.news.wisc.edu

Your students will find some great classroom discussion-starters at The Why Files, a site that examines the scientific angle of contemporary news stories and issues. Pages (with photos) take an in-depth look at particular topics of the day—from beach erosion to the latest cancer drug—with questions and integrated Web links along the way. An engaging site for students and teachers alike.

Cool Science

http://www.pbs.org/saf/5_cool/5_cool.html

This built-for-fun site is related to the Scientific American Frontiers series on PBS. Kids can delve into interactive sections such as the "Science Thing," a "Don't-Try-This-at-Home" experiment, a "Cyber Field Trip," and more. They can also check out "Cool Careers in Science," or participate in an online opinion poll. Further, there are pages of related resources and additional information about the Scientific American Frontiers programs.

How Stuff Works

http://www.howstuffworks.com

Like it says, this busy site explains in clear, readable text just how things work—from car engines to caffeine to cruise missiles. Categories include "Around the House," "Computers," "Automotive," "Your Teeth," "Food," "Electronics," "In the News"—and that's just for starters. The home page also features a "Question of the Day." This award-winning site was created by Marshall Brain, the author of 10 books (including *The Teenager's Guide to the Real World*) and a member of the Academy of Outstanding Teachers.

The Mad Scientist Network

http://www.madsci.org

The Mad Scientist Network offers learners the "collective craniums" of scientists and educators, in a virtual classroom where over 10,000 answered questions are stored in the online archive. The archive offers question-and-answer texts for a broad range of science subjects, including agriculture, anatomy, astronomy, cell biology, science history, and much more. Once in the archive section, teachers can generate a list of questions based on the grade level of those who submitted science questions. A great place for research.

Eisenhower National Clearinghouse—Science Lessons and Activities

http://www.enc.org/classroom/lessons/nf_lessci.htm

A straightforward page of lesson plans, projects, and science education links from the Eisenhower National Clearinghouse for Mathematics and Science Education. The larger

Eisenhower site (http://www.enc.org) includes a section of integrated science and math lessons, as well as a resource finder. Another interesting feature of the ENC online is the "Digital Dozen," a monthly list of 12 quality math and science Web sites.

The Science Club
http://www.halcyon.com/sciclub/

If you need information about how to begin a science fair in your school, ideas for science projects, and a source for science-education products, check out The Science Club. Other features include a list of "Ask Science Questions" sites, a page of "Fun Science" sites, and links to other science projects published on the Web.

Science/Nature for Kids
http://kidscience.miningco.com/kidsteens/ktschool/kidscience/

An in-depth tour of science topics, from animals and earth science to puzzles and zoos, with recommended school projects and science articles. There are also links to the larger About.com information search site, as well as a moderated online "chat" for kids.

Science Educational Gateway (SEGway)—Lesson List
http://cse.ssl.berkeley.edu/segway/master.html

A gold mine of science sites for K–12 teachers and students. Hotlinked sites include the Best of the Solar System, Geography From Space, Big Trouble in Earthquake Country, Sunspots, Rainbows and Spectra, and much more. Jump in!

 # SPACE

StarChild: A Learning Center for Young Astronomers
http://starchild.gsfc.nasa.gov/docs/StarChild/StarChild.html

Here's a super resource from NASA for young skygazers, and a great support site for educators who teach about the planets, the stars, and our solar system. There are really two sites here—Level 1 has information for the upper primary grades, while Level 2 gives more detailed information written for the middle school level. The site also contains links to Imagine the Universe, an astronomy site for ages 14 and older. StarChild contains clearly written explanations of important phenomena (orbits, particles, atmosphere, and so on). Other data and question-and-answer links are available throughout the site.

The Galileo Project

http://es.rice.edu/ES/humsoc/Galileo

For middle school students and older, The Galileo Project uses the visual analogy of Galileo's villa to organize information about the astronomer's life. By clicking on a map of Galileo's virtual villa, students can learn a good deal about the man and the time in which he lived. In "Family Quarters," there is information about Galileo's family; "Observing Terrace" contains accounts of Galileo's sightings of Jupiter's moons, while the "Chapel" holds a history of the Inquisition and biographies of major church figures of the day. There's a notable section, "Galileo's Daughter," which has English-language translations of letters Galileo received from his daughter, a nun in Italy's San Matteo convent. Other interesting sections include "Maps of Galileo's World," a "Timeline of Galileo's Life & Era," and "Student Work." Downloading is a bit slow, but it's well worth the time.

NASA's Quest Project

http://quest.arc.nasa.gov/

Another gift from NASA, the Quest Project Web site pools the resources of numerous projects, and many scientists, in one spot for easy access. Classrooms can sign up to participate in collaborative scientific projects, join ongoing chats with scientists, and enter a contest to help design a colony on Mars. Teachers exploring this site should also check "Bring the Internet Into Your Classroom" page, and within that, "Online Education Resources" (http://quest.arc.nasa.gov/OER/), for a wealth of additional school-sponsored and NASA-sponsored Web sites.

Project Galileo: Bringing Jupiter to Earth

http://www.jpl.nasa.gov/galileo

With the help of NASA's Jet Propulsion Laboratory, this site lets you follow the travels of the *Galileo* spacecraft, view photos sent by the *Hubble* telescope, investigate an area of K–12 resources, and much more. There are many pages of beautiful images, a "Frequently Asked Questions" page, information about Jupiter's moons, and a section about the *Galileo* spacecraft itself. An easy-to-use site for students and teachers.

A Mystery of Space: Stars

http://library.thinkquest.org/25763/

This student-created site is all about stars, with some innovative design features to help students visualize the night sky. "The Planetarium" has an interactive viewer that requires your computer to have a Java-enabled Web browser. (The latest versions of most browsers have this software feature already built-in, but if yours does not, there are links on the site that will allow you to download a version for free.) There are online "movies" and sections for user-submitted art, pictures, and myths about the cosmos.

► VOLCANOES

Volcano World

http://volcano.und.edu

Here is a well-organized site with lots of information and activities—all about volcanoes. There are many resources here to support any lesson about volcanoes, including "Ask a Vulcanologist," "Current Eruptions," and a "Teaching and Learning" section (with lessons, a review of types of volcanoes, volcano facts, and links). For children, there's a "Kids' Door" section, with "Legends about Volcanoes," "School Project Ideas," "Virtual Field Trips," and "Games & Fun Stuff." Another useful feature is "Today in Volcano History," a hyperlinked calendar.

Volcanoes Online

http://library.thinkquest.org/17457/

Volcanoes Online bills itself as "your ultimate guide to volcanoes on the Net," and it's not an idle boast. Students can learn about plate tectonics, types of volcanoes, types of eruptions, and the structure of volcanoes. The site also includes review questions, games, comics, and a virtual "Trip to Guatemala." Students designed this site for the international ThinkQuest competition, winning first prize in the interdisciplinary category for 1998.

Volcano Lovers

http://whyfiles.news.wisc.edu/031volcano/

Students visiting this site learn that the loudest sound on Earth "was not heavy metal," but Indonesia's Krakatau volcano, which exploded with the force of thousands of atomic bombs. This easy-to-read site gives clear explanations of volcanoes and related phenomena, a history of volcanic eruptions, an overview of volcano types, and a bibliography. Good for grades 5–7.

Volcanoes

http://pubs.usgs.gov/volc/cover2.html

This site is actually the online version of a book about volcanoes, originally published on paper, from the U.S. Geological Survey. The "just the facts" approach presents a very thorough look at all things volcanic, from "Principle Types of Volcanoes" to "Submarine Volcanoes" to "Extraterrestrial Volcanoes." A "Suggested Reading" page is included. (The home page also provides information about ordering the print version of the book.)

 # WEATHER

Scholastic Weather Center Resources

http://teacher.scholastic.com/fieldtrip/science/weather.htm

Scholastic has assembled a useful collection of articles and activities to help support teaching about weather, including materials on global climate, air patterns, floods, and a section where kids' questions are answered. While you're on the Scholastic Network, check out a unit on Hurricanes, at http://www.teacher.scholastic.com/hurrican/index.htm. From this page, your class can learn how to track a hurricane, read the writings of a hurricane specialist, explore related links, and more.

Dan's Wild Wild Weather Page

http://www.whnt19.com/kidwx/

From Dan Satterfield, meteorologist at WHNT-TV (Huntsville, Alabama), this site for kids ages 6–16 includes a long list of topics, from El Niño to precipitation. There's even a "Cloud Boutique" where visitors can view unusual cloud formations. The "For Teachers" section offers teaching units on weather and links that include How Weather Works and Weather and Climate Educational Resources.

The NOAA Central Library

http://www.lib.noaa.gov/docs/education.html

The National Oceanic and Atmospheric Administration (NOAA), the federal agency that studies and tracks our oceans and atmosphere, has put together a huge—and very complete—collection of links to sites filled with materials for teachers and students. Every aspect of weather and climatic data can be found through the links on this long page, as well as a series of ocean sites. There are also forecast sites for many (but not all) individual states, a listing of education sites from non-profit organizations, and many, many other sites. While you're looking through government-sponsored resources, take a peek at the "National Weather Service Education Outreach" page at http://www.nws.noaa.gov/om/edures.htm. There you'll find even more resources for K–12 students and educators.

The Hurricane Hunters

http://www.hurricanehunters.com/welcome.htm

This site tells the story of the 53rd Weather Reconnaissance Squadron (known as the Hurricane Hunters), whose pilots fly right into the eye of hurricanes to gather information and images of hurricanes and tropical storms. The "Homework Help" page contains a list of useful resources, hurricane facts, and other information for students.

▶ ENVIRONMENT

The Earth Day Groceries Project
http://www.earthdaybags.org/

A local event that virtually any school can launch, this project is spreading fast across the country. In 1998, nearly 500 schools participated; in 1999, the number doubled to over 1,000. This simple activity involves asking your local grocer (one that has paper bags on hand) to lend your class or school enough paper bags for each child. The students decorate the bags with environmental messages ("Save Our Earth," "Reduce, Reuse, and Recycle," and so on) and drawings, such as pictures of the Earth or trees. The decorated bags are returned to the grocer, who uses them to bag groceries on Earth Day (April 22nd). The site includes examples of decorated bags, as well as a "Starter Kit," a project summary, and other practical information. If your neighborhood grocer does not use paper bags, but is willing to distribute the bags you provide, contact: Shine2@ix.netcom.com.

The Web site also keeps a tally of the number of bags that have been decorated across the U.S., and you can log in and send your classroom's bag count as well. A nationwide report is available via an interactive map on the site.

Participating in this program has several benefits: It can open a classroom discussion on paper vs. plastic and other environmental conservation issues, it helps form a relationship with a local business, and the project is the type of school-community partnership that local newspapers like to cover.

Earth Day
http://earthday.wilderness.org/

This site, sponsored by the Wilderness Society, provides information for teachers and children about Earth Day. Here you will find a history of Earth Day, a "Teacher's Lounge" with a discussion forum, as well as kids' activities. Students can follow Migratory Max, the American Gold Plover, on his migratory path. There is an "Earth Day Quiz," a print-and-color section, and more.

EEK! Environmental Education for Kids!
http://www.dnr.state.wi.us/org/caer/ce/eek/

Environmental Education for Kids (EEK!) is an electronic magazine for students in grades 4–8, filled with facts, activities, "Cool Stuff," and riddles. The site includes a teacher's section with a group of teaching activities related to wildlife and environmental topics.

Access Excellence

http://www.accessexcellence.org/

Access Excellence is an exceptional site, offering a diverse selection of science-related material organized in a teacher-friendly structure. Sections include "Activities Exchange," "About Biotech," "Let's Collaborate," "Teaching Communities," "Classrooms of the 21st Century," and the "What's New" area. Further, the "Activities-to-Go" section includes the National Science Education Content Standards Directory, with links from each content standard to related activities on the site.

Your Community Environmental Quality Rating (E.Q.R.)

http://www.accessexcellence.org/ae/atg/released/0291-JonFiorella/index.html

One of the best ways for kids to understand environmental science is to begin at "home"—in their own community. This lesson helps students approach science as inquiry and to see the personal and social perspectives in science. It reinforces the idea that people can make a positive difference in their environment.

The E.Q.R. is a printable ratings sheet, using Westchester County, New York, as a model. Part 1 asks students to begin with a score of 100 points, and subtract a certain number of points depending on the degree of pollution (for example, "Subtract one additional point for each smog alert you had during the last year. Score____"). Part 2 involves student research on the local initiatives (such as recycling or park clean-up campaigns). Students add points for every positive action taken by the town government or community to come up with a final E.Q.R. rating.

Following Up:

This lesson addresses Westchester County, New York, and notes its unique location, with New York City to the south and the Hudson River to the west. In adapting this E.Q.R. to your area, have students think about the geographic characteristics they would include—is their town near a beach, a state park, or another distinctive natural resource or habitat?

BIOLOGY

Living Things
http://www.fi.edu/tfi/units/life

This site, supported by the Franklin Institute, is a tour of the basic biology curriculum—a survey of plants and animals as individuals, families, in neighborhoods, and in the grand "circle of life." All the information is presented in language your students can understand. Users can view the latest edition of the online *SciTech Newswire* to check science news, while *Science Update* and *Why Is It?* provide the latest on life science. Teachers can help themselves to the "Teacher Tips" area, and there is a "Keyword Index" to aid the search function.

Cool Science for Curious Kids
http://www.hhmi.org/coolscience/

Why are snakes like lizards and monkeys like moose? These and other burning kids' questions are explored here at Cool Science for Curious Kids, a biology site brought to us by the Howard Hughes Medical Institute (not be confused with the Cool Science site on the PBS Web site). The site is designed to pique the curiosity of youngsters, and the kid-friendly graphics and topics should immediately pull them in.

Access Excellence
http://www.accessexcellence.org/

There's much here to support teaching of biology, especially for the middle and high school grades. Outstanding features include "Access Excellence Collection/Activities Exchange," offering "The Mystery Spot" (interactive scientific mysteries for classroom use, developed to encourage student problem-solving), the "Fellows Collection" (a selection of biology classroom activities), "Activities-to-Go," a virtual "Teacher's Lounge," and a series of links to ongoing initiatives such as the National Human Genome Research Project, the Gene Connection Curriculum, the National Cancer Institute, and much more. Further, the site offers material about teaching bioethics, information on science and the media, a "Career Center," and its own search engine.

Neuroscience for Kids
http://weber.u.washington.edu/~chudler/neurok.html

It's hard to imagine how this subject could be made appealing to kids, but the site's designers have done it. Reaching out to students as well as teachers, Neuroscience for Kids contains

brightly colored pages with explanations and explorations of the brain and nervous system, experiments and activities, and a section where kids can ask questions of the "Neuroscientist Network," and find links to other resources. Students can also sign up to receive (via e-mail) the free *Neuroscience for Kids Newsletter*, while teachers can find their own "Resources for Teaching Neuroscience" page.

Digital Learning Center for Microbial Ecology— The Microbe Zoo

http://commtechlab.msu.edu/sites/dlc-me/

Everything you wanted to know about microbes is here, with sections including "The Microbe Zoo," "Microbe of the Month," "The Curious Microbe," "Microbes in the News"...need we say more? The Microbe Zoo, designed as a mini-theme park on your screen, has great information in a digestible format. Areas in the Zoo include "Dirtland," "Water World," "Animal Pavilion," "Snack Bar," and "Space Adventure." The more digitally adventurous teacher can check out Cells Alive! (http://www.cellsalive.com) where, with the help of QuickTime™ and a late-model Web browser, a classroom computer can run movies of cells in action and of viruses being destroyed, accompanied by relevant text and links.

How Stuff Works—Your Body

http://howstuffworks.com/category-body.htm

From the wonderful How Stuff Works site, students get clear answers to the mysteries of various bodily functions and reactions, such as how cells work, why skin tans (or burns), how poison ivy causes a rash, how sleep works, the sense of smell, and much more.

Bugs & Insects

http://teacher.scholastic.com/researchtools/articlearchives/bugs/index.htm

By posing questions that are always of interest to kids—"Insect or Spider? How Do You Tell?"— this resource page on bugs and insects contains materials to help teachers compile engaging lessons on these topics. Activities and other links are included.

The Development of Insect Flight

http://hannover.park.org/Canada/Museum/insects/insects.html

With an on-screen bee as your guide, this educational exhibit offers information on pages like "Insects in the Big Picture," "What Did Insects Come From?," "How Insects Fly," and "The Evolution of Flight." Pictures and links help tell the stories. This site is part of Canada's Hooper

Reviled and Revered

http://educate.si.edu/resources/lessons/siyc/herps/

Another gift from the Smithsonian, here's a free, online unit all about those fascinating creatures classified as "herps"— toads, turtles, frogs, crocodiles, salamanders, and many other amphibians and reptiles. There's an introduction discussing how people have viewed herps, followed by five lessons (with extension activities), and a resources page. Lessons include a look at students' attitudes toward these creatures, a quick survey of how various cultures have portrayed herps, an art project, a writing activity, and an exercise in which students are encouraged to design their own exhibit.

NetVet—The Electronic Zoo

http://netvet.wustl.edu/ssi.htm

If you are looking for a one-stop index of links to all things animal, here it is. There are more links here than you can count, from the sublime (scholarly associations and serious journals) to the ridiculous (American Fraternal Order of Lizard Lovers). But there are many sites linked to specific animals (including dinosaurs and fictional animals). There is also a list of commercial sites for those seeking to purchase books and supplies.

For the Birds

http://www.inhs.uiuc.edu/chf/pub/virtualbird/educational.html

What makes a bird a bird? A visit to this site will make the answer clear. It includes 12 lessons for students that are packed with information and diagrams, as well as companion lesson plans for teachers. Each of the teacher lesson plans includes grade-level information, objectives, and standard correlations. This is a straightforward and very easy-to-use site.

Virtual Frog Dissection Kit

http://george.lbl.gov/ITG.hm.pg.docs/dissect/info.html

Were you that squeamish student who couldn't bear to dissect a frog? This site allows for the virtual, interactive dissection of a frog, in a number of languages. Part of the "Whole Frog" online project, students can get inside Fluffy the Frog to see what a frog is all about; further, kids can test their knowledge playing the "Virtual Frog Builder Game." This page allows you to link to an area of frog statistics as well as a government-sponsored frog and toad monitoring system called Frogwatch. Related frog and biology links are also included.

Discovering Dinosaurs

http://dinosaurs.eb.com/

From Encyclopaedia Britannica, here's an informative site for upper primary and middle school students about the dinosaur's environment, anatomy, behavior, and physiology. Students can trace the "great dinosaur debate" through time by clicking on squares in a color-coded, themed grid. There are also links to resources and information on where to find books about this popular subject.

Dinosaurs & Fossils
http://teacher.scholastic.com/researchtools/articlesarchive/dino/index.htm

A comprehensive package of classroom materials, with many articles and activities designed to spark inquiry, discussion, and research into the fascinating world of dinosaurs. Topics range from "Why Did Dinosaurs Become Extinct?" to "Dinosaurs of Argentina." You'll also find a section called "Answers to Kids' Questions" that looks into specifics such as physical characteristics (dinosaur teeth, diet, claws), flying reptiles, and more.

Dinosauria On-Line
http://www.dinosauria.com/

It's hard to gauge the number of resources available on this site by looking at its overly simple home page. But clicking onto the "Full Index Page" lays it all out, and with a single click you can get to the "Dinosaur Picture Gallery," the "Omnipedia," and more.

 GEOLOGY

Rocks and Minerals
http://www.fi.edu/efi/units/rocks/rocks.html

This site offers a good, no-nonsense approach to the subject of rocks and minerals, with explanations of terms (sedimentary, igneous, and so on), and related links to geological resources online. There are additional links to relevant lessons, graphics, teaching resources, and online museum collections and exhibits, which help demonstrate the information explained in the text. This instructional unit is part of the larger Franklin Institute Web site.

Minerals, Crystals, and Gems: Stepping-Stones to Inquiry
http://educate.si.edu/resources/lessons/siyc/gems/

From *Smithsonian in Your Classroom* online, this all-in-one unit offers an introductory essay, three lessons (with images), and a page of resources. Designed for grades 3–8, this site is a good place to begin if your students are new to the subjects of minerals, gems, and crystals, or if you are just looking for some solid lesson plans on these subjects.

Geologylink
http://www.geologylink.com

Here is a central resource of sites rich in geology information for students, teachers, and academics. Learners can use the "Virtual Classroom" section to link to online geology courses across the globe. Other features include "The Earth Today" (geologic events), "Geology in the News," and "Inside Geology," which is a link to hundreds of class lectures, Web sites, glossaries, and organizations. Educational publisher Houghton Mifflin sponsors the site.

Rock Hounds With Rocky

http://www.fi.edu/fellows/payton/rocks/

This award-winning site, designed for the primary grades, is an Internet tour of rock collecting, basic geology knowledge, puzzles, and other resources. Goodies for teachers include lesson plans, recommended literature, and an activities collection. The mascot of this site is Rocky the hound, who sports a miner's helmet and presents a friendly image to kids.

Neill's Geology: Ask-a-Geologist

http://www.geocities.com/Athens/Parthenon/8991/askme.html

Like it says, here is a place for geology questions great and small. Inquiries and answers are posted in clearly written text. Users can submit their questions via a form on the home page, and answers are posted on the site.

 OCEAN LIFE

Where Is It Like Where You Live? Temperate Oceans

http://www.mobot.org/MBGnet/salt/oceans/index.htm

Temperate Oceans is an omnibus site about the seas and everything in them, with extensive information about ocean animals, as well as sections such as "Data," "Frequently Asked Questions," "How the Ocean Refreshes Itself," "Dolphin-Safe Tuna," and other topics and links. From this page, learners can click onto the "Tropical Oceans" page (with information about coral reefs) or the "Shorelines" area. Good information is included here, especially in the "Ocean Animals" section.

Ocean Planet: Educational Materials

http://seawifs.gsfc.nasa.gov/OCEAN_PLANET/HTML/search_educational_materials.html

An amazing collection of links about our oceans, inspired by the Smithsonian's *Ocean Planet* exhibit. The links are divided into "Teacher Materials," "Fact Sheets," "Family Activities," "Children's Books," "Theater Scripts," and "CD-ROMs." Educators should enjoy the wealth of materials accessible via this page—the first link in the teacher's section is an online curriculum kit from the Smithsonian, with lesson plans, activities, and teacher answer keys.

Whale Songs

http://whales.ot.com

Whale Songs is at once an informational site about whales and an interesting journey of exploration, written by Lance Leonhardt, an American science teacher. Leonhardt sailed through the Azores on the research vessel *Song of the Whale*, and the viewer is presented with a clickable map on the home page that allows access to his diary entries. There are informational links and audio files throughout his writings, making for a very interactive Web experience. The site also offers "Cetacean Info," "Educational Resources," and a section about the *Song of the Whale*.

Educational Resources—Sea World

http://www.seaworld.org/teacherguides/teacherguides.html

A collection of teacher's guides with recommended grade levels. Online units include "Ocean Olympians" (grades 4–8), "Water" (grades 4–8), "Flight for Survival" (grades 2–8), and more, with some related links to other resources and programs.

Whales: A Thematic Web Unit

http://curry.edschool.virginia.edu/go/Whales/

This site will support any lesson about whales you are teaching. It includes recommended student activities involving whale research, language arts, math, social studies, critical thinking, and, of course, science. There is a section called "Project Ideas," as well as a "Project Gallery." Additional goodies include a bibliography, book reviews, a listing of places for class field trips, homework suggestions, and lesson plans. Beyond this is a very formidable collection of Internet resources on whales.

Whales of the World Educational Program

http://iwc.org/teachers_kit/tguide.html

For the upper primary grades, Whales of the World offers 11 activities based on knowledge of whales, including "Body Parts of a Whale," "Games," "Whale Migration," and "History of Whaling," as well as related mathematics, writing, and art activities. There is a separate "Teachers' Activity Guide" on the site, offering notes and suggestions for using Whales of the World in class. This site is a project of the International Wildlife Coalition.

 # MATTER AND ENERGY

Chem4Kids!

http://www.chem4kids.com/

Probably the most fun chemistry site for upper elementary and middle schoolers you'll ever see. There's plenty of clearly written, kid-friendly information here on topics such as matter, elements, atoms, math, and reactions. Newcomers can take a virtual tour, while an on-site search engine helps the user locate topics. Chemistry quizzes help with content review. If you're looking for a way to get your students interested in chemistry, the elements, or matter, make this site your first stop.

It's Electric!

http://www.mos.org/sln/toe/toe.html

Developed by the Boston Museum of Science, the Theater of Electricity offers historical and biographical information about inventions and inventors, science background for teachers, and hands-on activities.

Part
2

Social Studies

 ## GENERAL RESOURCES

National Council for the Social Studies
http://www.ncss.org/

You can review the social studies standards by visiting this site. You'll also find lesson plans, research, and other resources for teachers here.

 ## GEOGRAPHY

National Geographic Xpeditions
http://www.nationalgeographic.com/xpeditions/home.html

If you've been looking for that "one-stop-shopping" geography site, this is about as good as it gets. National Geographic Xpeditions offers the complete texts of the U.S. National Geography Standards, with links to lessons and activities that put these concepts into hands-on classroom practice. In the "Standards" section, clicking on a specific standard opens up a full exposition of each idea, as well as "Education" and "Family Xpeditions" grouped by grade levels

(K–4, 5–8, 9–12). Additionally, over 1,800 map views (printable), as well as interactive explorations in its "Xpedition Hall," can keep you (and your students) busy for hours. From the Xpeditions main page, you can link out to Geography Education (http://www.nationalgeographic.com/education), a related site designed for teachers. Along with offering more classroom ideas and a faculty forum, there is a link to National Geographic's wonderful Map Machine, where all manner of maps can be found. This entire site is really a treasure chest of geographical knowledge. You can also go to the home of *National Geographic* on the Web, at http://www.nationalgeographic.com, to preview its well-known magazine, and link to *National Geographic's World*, the children's magazine.

Geography and Culture of China (Activity: A Cooperative Map)
http://www.askasia.org/frclasrm/lessplan/l000049.htm

This page offers a series of classroom activities related to the study of China at the middle school level. However, the first activity, "A Cooperative Map," can be applied to any country. In this exercise, students demonstrate the ability to work within a cooperative group to draw, label, and color a large-scale map of China. Responsibilities and topics, such as research, drawing, locating physical features, man-made features, provinces, and so on, are assigned to individuals within the group. Students use longitude and latitude lines as a guide for locations on the map. The oversized map can be displayed in the school when it is finished. Further, students can be given comprehension questions related to the map at completion. This page is part of the larger AskAsia Web site, at http://www.askasia.org, a K–12 Asian studies clearinghouse developed and maintained by the Asia Society.

The Learning Web
http://www.usgs.gov/education

This is a section of the vast U.S. Geological Survey Web site focusing on K–12 education, and there is no shortage of good information and lesson plans here. "Teaching in the Learning Web" has activities and lessons for the classroom, while "Living in the Learning Web" looks at topics that affect people in everyday life. Sections in "Teaching in the Learning Web" include "Changing World" (information about rocks, tree rings, and other signs of how the Earth has changed over time), "Working with Maps" (explaining about various types of maps, with related lessons), and "Earth Hazards" (volcanic eruptions and other earth-shaking phenomena). A good way to start: click on the "Index of Lessons and Activities."

Five Times Five: Five Activities for Teaching Geography's Five Themes
http://www.education-world.com/a_lesson/lesson071.shtml

From the award-winning Education World site, here are recommended activities to help educators teach the five themes of geography: location, place, human/environmental interaction, movement, and regions. The clearly written text is filled with great ideas, adaptable across a wide student age range. This is a very useful resource, with links to related articles within the Education World site.

National Atlas of the United States

http://www-atlas.usgs.gov/scripts/start.html

Although the home page is slow to download, the wealth of information on this interactive site is worth waiting for. At first, the site offers an outline of the United States; at the right, there are columns that offer a menu of views across a diverse range of topics, including "Distribution of Butterflies and Moths" (by types), "Boundaries" (counties, Indian lands, and so on), "Environment," "People," "Transportation," and more. To view maps that show selected information, users choose from the menu column and click to download the newly layered map. Users can also zoom in or out of specific parts of the map, making them appear larger or smaller. This site uses frames, so it is recommended for those using either Netscape 3.0 or Microsoft Internet Explorer 3.0 or later. (Note: at this writing, both Web browsers were available in much newer versions, so even if your browser is about two years old, you should be able to use this site.)

The National Park Pages

http://www.geocities.com/Yosemite/9173/national_parks.html

This site, the winner of the Yosemite's Pride Award, is a virtual tour of our nation's most spectacular geologic wonders, our national parks. From the beginning page, the viewer can tour Yosemite, Sequoia National Park, Joshua Tree National Park, and more. There is also a link to the Manzanar National Historic Site, a camp where Japanese-American citizens were interned during World War II.

STUDYING THE STATES

Stately Knowledge

http://www.ipl.org/youth/stateknow/

Your fourth, fifth, and sixth graders will be very happy to learn about this site, an easy-to-use compendium of facts about all 50 states. The home page presents a simple listing of states, as well as links to charts that show comparisons of size and population, the date that each state joined the Union, and links to resources and games. Clicking on the name of a state presents learners with a simple list that includes the state's capital, population, current governor, state motto, and the origin of its name. Of course, the state flower, bird, and flag are also included, along with other data.

Flag Tag!

http://www.un.org/Pubs/CyberSchoolBus/flagtag/

Here is a fun and simple game from the United Nation's CyberSchoolBus Web site that asks students to match countries to their flags. Students can either pick a country from a menu of choices, or have the Web site pick one at random. Once the choice is made, the screen presents the student with three flags from countries around the world, but only one of them can be the real flag of the country. Take a guess!

50 States and Capitals

http://www.50states.com/

This site is packed with facts about each of the 50 states. Students can view the state flags and easily gather other information here.

 # ANCIENT CIVILIZATIONS

Daily Life in Ancient Rome

http://members.aol.com/Donnclass/Romelife.html

One of a series of Web units on ancient cultures prepared by Donald G. Donn of Corkran Middle School in Maryland. This easy-to-read page provides students with an understandable view of what life was like in ancient Rome—from the type of breakfast people ate to what types of houses they lived in. There are lesson plans, and links to Rome-related sites and those of other cultures.

The Romans (from the BBC)

http://www.bbc.co.uk/education/romans/index.shtml

The material on this site, subtitled "Investigating the Romans," is a very solid teacher resource about the ancient republic and its people. Topics include "Who Were the Romans?", "The City of Rome," "Roman Technology," "Education in Rome," "Leisure," and much more. An interactive quiz is also available on the site.

Europe/Russia/Eastern Europe—Ancient/Classical European History

http://www.crosswinds.net/~dboals/class.html

Here is an omnibus collection of resources that will help you explore just about anything you wanted to know about early Europe, from prehistoric times through the Classical Period. Information categories begin at "Prehistory," and proceed through "Urban History," "Map Resources for Ancient/Classical Europe," "Science-Philosophy-Religion," "Art-Architecture-

Drama-Literature," "War and Conflict," and beyond. You probably won't need everything offered via this page, but it's a good place to begin information gathering. This page is part of the larger History/Social Studies Web site for K–12 Teachers, at http://www.execpc.com/~dboals/boals.html.

Mr. Donn's Units: Early & Classical Greece

http://members.aol.com/DonnAnCiv/Greece.html

Another wonderful Web unit from Donald G. Donn of Corkran Middle School in Maryland. Teachers should begin with the "Unit Overview" for the rationale, objectives, and assessment ideas. There's quite a bit of material here, ranging from "Minos & Mycenae," through "Rise of City States," "Daily Life," "Greek Culture," "Greek Gods," and "Wars," to vocabulary lists and fun activities. Take a look!

Alexander the Great (Alexander III of Macedon)

http://1stmuse.com/frames/index.html

This Web site is a very good, informative source for educators about Alexander the Great. Created by John J. Popovic, who has dedicated his site to "the most charismatic and heroic king of all times," the on-site materials are organized in a sensible way via a right-hand frame. The contents cover Alexander's origins, his fabulous conquests from Europe to India, the story of Alexander's death, a general overview of the Hellenistic Era, a bibliography, and related links.

Ancient Greece

http://home1.gte.net/paterfam/ancientgreecesplash.htm

This site is a teacher-designed resource with lessons and quizzes about ancient Greece. Topics include "Introduction to Gods and Goddesses," "Geography," "Art and Architecture," "Homer's Odyssey," "Big Bad Boats," "Hercules," and "Myths and More." Teacher's tools include "Course Description/Overview," "Prerequisite Skills," "Learner Outcome," "Grading Rubric," and "Materials." After the home page is fully loaded on screen, some original electronic music plays (and repeats, until you click to another page).

Early People of the Western Hemisphere

http://www.kamalii.k12.hi.us/Early_People_Of_The_Wester.html

This resource page offers a collection of hard-to-find educational sites about the first peoples of the Americas, including the Aztec, Maya, Anasazi, and Inca. It also offers some suggested activities and links to Web site lesson plans on these civilizations.

The Aztecs of Mexico—Student Teacher Resource Center

http://northcoast.com/~spdtom/aztec.html

A good resource for information about the ancient Aztec civilization of Mexico, this area is part of the larger Aztecs of Mexico Home Page site, at http://northcoast.com/~spdtom/index.html.

Clicking on the Aztec link brings up a menu that includes "Religion," "Medicine," "Rulers," "Features," "Links," and more. The "Aztec Rulers" page (very long) has a wealth of information about Aztec history, including a chronology of the people, a list of Aztec rulers, and synopses of their reigns.

The Mississippian and Late Prehistoric Period

http://www.cr.nps.gov/seac/misslate.htm

An informative essay from the Southeastern Archeological Center (or SEAC, in Tallahassee, Florida), with images and links related to ancient Mississippian societies thought to have stretched from around East St. Louis, Illinois, southward to the Mississippi basin. The text spans several topics, including burial mounds (flat-top pyramids) and the locations of Mississippian cultures in the midwestern and southern U.S. This site can be paired with Monumental American Indian Architecture, at http://www.cr.nps.gov/delta/mounds.htm, which provides brief descriptions of the various burial mounds and temple complexes found in the lower Mississippi Delta, and links to other sites with Native American–built mounds. You and your class can also view artwork and other artifacts from Mississipian culture, specifically from the powerful Cahokia tribe of the Midwest, on the Mississippian Civilization (900–1750 AD) site, at http://www.hp.uab.edu/omage_archive.up/upi.html. Photos on the page are "thumbnails"— clicking them will bring up an enlarged image.

Ancient Egypt

http://www.kent.wednet.edu/curriculum/soc_studies/Egypt/egypt.html

This uncomplicated site offers many informational pages about the history and culture of ancient Egypt. Material is grouped chronologically (Pre-Dynastic through the New Kingdom), and there is a page of lesson ideas for use in class. The texts on these Web pages contain hotlinks to related pages. Illustrative images support the texts.

Ancient Egypt (from the Core Values Internet Resource Library)

http://webtest.ousd.k12.ca.us/foundations
/curric_library/egypt/egypt_index.html

This Web page, from an online series by the Oakland Unified School District, offers carefully selected Web resources designed to supplement and extend a sixth-grade unit on ancient Egypt and the Kingdom of Kush. Topics include "Art and Architecture," "Writing and Mathematics," "Culture and Daily Life," "Mythology and Religion," as well as pages of resources on the Kingdom of Kush. Considering the range of resources, the material may be adapted easily for slightly older or younger classes.

Daily Life in Ancient Egypt

http://members.aol.com/Donnclass/Egyptlife.html

Teacher Donald G. Donn of Corkran Middle School in Maryland has created a student-friendly look at life in old Egypt. Kids can read an introduction to Egyptian society, learn some interesting Egyptian trivia, and gather information about Egyptian tombs. Online lessons and links are provided.

Lesson Plan—Papyrus

http://members.aol.com/WERedu/PlanEg1.html

If you're teaching about ancient Egypt, you will be interested in this lesson about papyrus from Wide Horizons Resources of San Diego, California. Along with some basic data on the way writing scrolls were made from papyrus, there are student assignments, teacher's notes, and an assessment rubric. "Teacher's Notes" will guide you through working with students to develop historic and geographic literacy, language skills, critical thinking, and basic studies skills. Teachers can also order papyrus imported from Egypt via this site. A link to a more basic lesson suitable for ESL students or grades 5–6 is available at: http://members.aol.com/WERedu /PlanEg1Basic.html.

Mr. Donn's Unit on Ancient Mesopotamia

http://members.aol.com/DonnAnCiv/mesounit.html

Here's a thorough teaching unit on early Mesopotamian civilization, with an in-depth "Unit Overview," and sections including "Geography," "Agriculture," "Religion & Epics," "Cuneiform," "Inventions," "Daily Life," "Hammurabi's Code," and more. You can also access the tests and reviews at the end of the section.

Mesopotamia (From the Core Values Internet Resource Library)

http://webtest.ousd.k12.ca.us/foundations/curric_library/meso/meso_index.html

This site includes another useful menu of links from the Core Values Internet Library, courtesy of the Oakland Unified School District. From this page, teachers can access various educational Web sites related to ancient Mesopotamia, covering the following subject areas: Religion and Epics, Educational Projects, General Resources, Lecture Notes, and Images and Multimedia.

Ancient Africa From the Beginnings

http://www.cocc.edu/cagatucci/classes/hum211/timelines/htimeline.htm

A serious and heavily researched site for educators on the subject of ancient Africa is presented here. Information is organized chronologically (beginning at 5 to 2.5 million B.C.) with a voluminous number of Web links to demonstrate the points on the timeline. There is extensive material here about the ancient African civilizations that rose around the Nile, including Nubia, Egypt, and Ethiopia. If you are preparing lessons on early African peoples and cultures, this is a treasure chest of materials. The end of this timeline is hotlinked to a successive chronology rich in resources on African Empires.

Indus Valley Civilization—A Social Studies/Language Arts Lesson

http://members.aol.com/WERedu/PlanIndia.html

Here is a wonderful, and very complete, lesson for middle school students about daily life and culture during the Harappan civilization. Students learn about this very early civilization by reading the online story *Life in the Indus Valley*, and then are given exercises that include a "Story Web," a travel brochure, and a guided reading. This online lesson plan, from Wide Horizons Resources in San Diego, California, is also available in a more basic version suitable for ESL or grades 5–6, at http://members.aol .com/WERedu/PlanIndiaBasic.html.

The Ancient Indus Valley

http://www.harappa.com/har/har0.html

This site is a fabulous introduction to the ancient Indus Valley civilization (also called the Harappan civilization), located in present-day southern Pakistan. Here, in one place, you (and your students) can view a 90-slide exhibit of artifacts and artwork from the Indus Valley, learn about Harappan writing, the great city of Mohenjo-Daro, and see other virtual exhibits. A "must" for classes learning about this significant civilization.

Rama and the Ramayana: Lessons in Dharma

http://www.askasia.org/frclasrm/lessplan/1000054.htm

Here you can find a synopsis of the *Ramayana*, a 3,000-year-old text and one of the oldest surviving epics from the ancient world. Further, a lesson plan is presented that gives a clear explanation of the concept of dharma, a central tenet of the Hindu and (many centuries later) Buddhist philosophies. The lesson is also linked to an illustrated version of the *Ramayana* that should keep students engaged for hours. To prepare for reading the *Ramayana*, be sure to click on the "Introduction" for a look at the central characters and their roles. These pages are part of the larger AskAsia Web site, located at http://www.askasia.org.

Asian Topics

http://www.columbia.edu/itc/eacp/asiasite/index.htm

From Columbia University's East Asia Curriculum Project, this well-researched site offers an excellent overview of important eras in Chinese and Japanese history. The home page offers a "split" screen of topics from China and Japan. The Chinese area includes pages such as "Confucian Teaching," "The Confucian Tradition," "Tang Poetry," and information about specific poets. The Japanese area offers sections such as "Classical Japan," "Medieval Japan," "Tokugawa Japan," and more. Classrooms with RealPlayer™ can see and hear prominent scholars talk briefly about each of these topics.

Ancient China

http://webtest.ousd.k12.ca.us/foundations/curric_library/china/china_history.html

This is a collection of general resource Web sites, selected to give teachers supporting material and background on the history and geography of ancient China. These links, including a chronology of ancient Chinese history, are from the Core Values Internet Resource Library of the Oakland Unified School District. It is linked to a collection of Silk Road sites for kids.

Golden Legacy

http://ericir.syr.edu/Projects/CHCP/index.html

The Golden Legacy is an award-winning curriculum on Chinese culture and the heritage of Chinese Americans. Although the full print edition of the curriculum contains 30 lessons, only three lessons were designed for third to fifth graders: "Bound Feet," "Abacus," and "Lunar Calendar." The lessons include handouts and visuals. The curriculum was created by the Chinese Historical and Cultural Project.

Who Invented It? When? Chinese Inventions

http://www.askasia.org/frclasrm/lessplan/1000019.htm

This site presents a fun introductory quiz on the contributions of Chinese civilization to the world. Students are asked to record where and when certain items were invented, including the wheelbarrow, paper money, the decimal system, the seismograph, matches, and so on. They may be surprised to learn that all these things originated in China a very long time ago. A teacher's answer key is provided.

Stories of the Dreaming

http://www.dreamtime.net.au/

The place we call Australia had a rich tapestry of cultures long before the first European settlers arrived. This remarkable Web site is an online exhibit that resulted from collaboration between Australia's Cultural Network and the Australian Museum. The stories come from the cultures of indigenous Australians and have been collected from all over Australia. The site offers insights into the roles of storytelling and dreaming in Aboriginal societies and provides a short online glossary of unfamiliar words. For each story, the user can choose to read the text only, to hear the storyteller, or select either low-resolution or high-quality video (depending on the capabilities of the user's computer). A very good window into a special world.

 EXPLORERS

Discoverers Web
http://www.win.tue.nl/cs/fm/engels/discovery/

Here is the granddaddy of all Web pages for information about explorers, with innumerable links covering explorers throughout history. From the Phoenicians to Commander Peary and beyond, it's all here, including an impressive array of links about non-Western explorers and cross-cultural forays into the unknown. Further, there is a separate page dedicated to Christopher Columbus, at http://www.win.tue.nl/cs/fm/engels/discovery/columbus.html, which can set your students on explorations of their own.

Columbus Day
http://deil.lang.uiuc.edu/web.pages/holiday/Columbus.html

Here's another one-stop resource dedicated to Christopher Columbus. From this page, learners can link to a timeline of Columbus's life, see maps of his voyages, view "Myths About Columbus," and get information about Columbus's ships. There are also excerpts from his journal, his letter to the King and Queen of Spain, and links to more Web pages. Moreover, there is an attempt to balance all available information by including a section called "Columbus Controversies." The site links to the Library of Congress exhibit, "1492, An Ongoing Voyage."

Viking Discoverers
http://www.win.tue.nl/cs/fm/engles/discovery/viking.html

A compendium of Viking Web listings, providing links to pages on everything from trading posts in Medieval Russia to artifacts found in North America. This very useful resource is part of the larger Discoverers Web site (see review at top of page).

Lewis & Clark: The Journey of the Corps of Discovery
http://www.pbs.org/lewisandclark/

This award-winning site, designed as a companion to the PBS documentary by Ken Burns, is easy to navigate and provides the historical context of Lewis and Clark's expeditions through the Northwest. Informative areas include the "Corps of Discovery," "Native Americans," "The Archive" (expedition timeline, maps, and journals), and "Living History," which features the perspectives of historians on Lewis and Clark. For teachers, there's "Classroom Resources," with 17 lesson plans, many of them tied to the National Council for the Social Studies teaching standards.

Discovering Lewis and Clark

http://www.lewis-clark.org/choice.htm

An intensely information-rich resource, with maps, firsthand accounts of meetings with Indian tribes, the perils of the journey, what the explorers had to eat, and much, much more. Tip: The beginning page is not very intuitive. To get started, you must scroll down near the bottom of the page and click on the "high bandwidth" or "low bandwidth" options (depending on the Web browser you are using) to enter the site. Once inside, learners can investigate the journey of Lewis and Clark via a series of drop-down menus presenting a choice of pathways including "The Expedition," "Journal Excerpts," or "Discovery Paths."

 # NATIVE AMERICANS

NativeTech

http://www.nativetech.org/NativeTech/

This is truly an unusual Web site, with the stated mission of "disconnecting the term 'primitive' from perceptions of Native American technology and art." Here is a vast labor of love, with extensive information about Native American practice in beadwork, feathers, clay and pottery, games, toys, weaving, food, poetry and stories, and more. There is a lot of good information here to supplement any lesson on Native American life or art. Take a peek at Native American History of Corn at http://www.nativeweb.org/cornhusk/cornhusk.html, a clearly written overview of how Native Americans systematically developed and cultivated maize from a less bountiful ancestral plant, as well as their multiple uses for the cornhusk.

First Nations Histories

http://www.dickshovel.com/Compacts.html

Here is a compendium of information about nearly 50 individual tribes (including those "recognized" and "unrecognized" by the U.S. government). The beginning page offers one-paragraph thumbnail sketches of tribal histories (U.S. and Canada); clicking on the name above each paragraph will bring up another page with information specific to the tribe. Further, the site offers "a critical re-evaluation" of Manifest Destiny and the geopolitical context in which the Northern Plains Indian Wars were undertaken.

First Americans for Grade Schoolers

http://www.u.arizona.edu/ic/kmartin/School/index.htm

Using this site, teachers can guide their upper elementary school students through interesting activities, explorations of native cultures, and tribal histories. The Teacher's Corner, accessible from the home page, is good place to begin (it provides a brief introduction and links to the various sections). Take a look at "Rethinking Indians," an exercise in examining cultural stereotypes.

Native American Geometry
http://www.earthmeasure.com/

Here is a thoughtful, interdisciplinary site taking a novel approach to understanding first peoples, multiculturalism, art, and geometry. The Education section (http://www.earthmeasure.com/Education/index.html) is divided into the "Introduction," "Concepts," "Books," and "Tests." Based on the premise that "when you do the art, math happens!", the exercises incorporate mathematical concepts that are necessary for the students to accomplish certain designs. Exercises offered on this site have been field tested on students from grades 2–9.

NativeWeb
http://www.nativeweb.org

At this site you'll find a compendium of resources by and for indigenous peoples in North and South America. There are links to information and Web pages about culture, books and music, and communities, as well as sub-categories including food, crafts, Native education, and information about various tribes across both continents. The contents are a mixed bag—if you are doing original research on specific tribes, crafts, or histories, you may have to dig a bit to find what you're after.

 # COLONIAL LIFE IN AMERICA

Colonial Williamsburg Foundation
http://www.history.org

The Colonial Williamsburg Foundation site offers information about this historic town, the state of Virginia, and eighteenth-century America. Resources include field trip information (actual and "electronic" field trips), as well as a useful section of classroom-tested lesson plans. Supporting materials are on the site, linked to lessons. Numerous primary source documents are available, including Declarations of the First Continental Congress and the Declaration of Independence, as well as biographical outlines of prominent early Americans.

The Stamp Act

Two lesson plans found on this site form a good foundation for teaching about the beginnings of the American Independence movement.

Lesson One: Colonial Reaction to the Stamp Act
http://www.history.org/other/teaching/tchcrone.htm

Americans living in colonies under the British crown were subject to the rulings and acts of the British Parliament, although they had no effective voice in the decisions that affected their lives. One very pivotal ruling was the Stamp Act of

1765, which galvanized resistance against British rule and against taxation without representation.

Lesson Two: Eighteenth-Century and Twentieth-Century Forms of Resistance
http://www.history.org/other/teaching/tchcrtwo.htm

In this lesson, students look at various forms of resistance employed by people during Colonial rule. It asks them to discuss those forms and compare them to the forms of resistance practiced in the twentieth century (e.g., the methods of Martin Luther King, Gandhi, and Vietnam War protesters).

Tar and Feathers in Revolutionary America
http://revolution.h-net.msu.edu/essays/irvin.feathers.html

This form of resistance, usually practiced against those who collected taxes on behalf of the British, started as a way to humiliate, rather than harm, its targets. What happened? Seventh and eighth grade students can find out by reading this essay.

Virtual Jamestown
http://jefferson.village.virginia.edu/vcdh/jamestown/

The goal of Virtual Jamestown is to present as much information as possible about what it must have been like for three very different groups of people to live alongside one another—English settlers, Native peoples, and African captives (who arrived in Jamestown in 1619). The site presents primary source documents (laws, census data, state papers, maps), accounts by modern-day historians, and a timeline. The Jamestown Resources section includes teaching materials, modern maps of Virginia, a bibliography, and links to other sites. "Jamestown in Time," under development at the time of this writing, will compare events in Jamestown with events happening in Europe, Africa, Asia, and South America during the same time period.

The People and the Land: The Wampanoag of Southern New England
http://www.plimoth.org/Library/Wampanoag/wampcolo.htm

The coast of Massachusetts, including the area that is now called Cape Cod, has been the historic home of the Wampanoag people. This account, written from the perspective of the first inhabitants of this land, details the influx of European visitors and settlers from about 1600, and the impact of events on the Wampanoag way of life. Good for sixth grade or older. This page is part of the larger Plimoth-on-Web site, created around a "living history" museum in Massachusetts. The entire "Library" section is worth looking at.

Montcalm and Wolfe—The French and Indian War
http://www.digitalhistory.org/wolfe.html

Here is a good overview of the people and places engaged in the seven-year-long French and Indian War, with information about two of its major leaders, as well as historical information including "A Prelude to War," "British Lake Vessels," "British Forts," "French Forts," "Major Battles," and a bibliography. A History Channel–recommended site.

Native American Clashes With European Settlers
http://www.wvlc.wvnet.edu/history/indland.html

This site provides synopses of Native American conflicts with Europeans, with a focus on the West Virginia, Virginia, and Ohio Valley regions. The information presented here is useful as teacher background material in preparing for a lesson about Indian-settler relations and history. The text includes a review of alliances, the Native American concept of land and land ownership, and British-Indian confederation during the Revolutionary War.

 # AMERICAN REVOLUTIONARY WAR

American Revolutionary War: Thematic Unit
http://people2.clarityconnect.com/webpages4/kcarsons/oconunit/index.htm

Here is a practical, step-by-step map of how to teach the American Revolution, with a 15-day plan designed to give students an understanding of the birth of our country. There are games, economic simulations, synopses of significant events (Boston Tea Party, etc.). This unit, authored by teacher Shannon O'Connor, targets grades 5–8 and makes good use of the Web, with informational links woven through the lessons.

The American Revolution and Colonial Times
http://library.advanced.org/10966/timeT.shtml

This project challenges students to imagine they have traveled back in time and entered colonial times. The class is divided into five stations, each offering a different experience that one would encounter in colonial days. Station examples include Colonial Music, Colonial Food, and Colonial Games. Students research and put together the stations. The site includes a printable worksheet on which students write their observations after visiting each station. Enjoy!

Explore the Amazing World of Early America

http://earlyamerica.com/earlyamerica/index.html

A very useful (and pretty) resource on Revolutionary America, containing links to reproductions of the Declaration of Independence, the Constitution, and the Bill of Rights (also offered in modern English). The "Milestone Events" section provides information on historical events that led to war; "Pages from the Past" allows users to view important writings, including Thomas Paine's *The Rights of Man*; and "Firsts" takes a look at the first newspaper, the first political cartoon, the first declaration of the Thanksgiving holiday, and more. There are biographies (actually, entire online books) of George Washington (written by his contemporary, David Ramsey), and Daniel Boone, and Ben Franklin's autobiography. This site also contains maps and a gallery of early American portraits.

Early American History Interactive Crossword Puzzle

http://earlyamerica.com/crossword/index.html

A crossword puzzle is a fun way to measure your students' knowledge of early Americana. The puzzles can be played either on the computer or printed out. The site also provides access to previous crossword puzzles on the same subject.

The American Revolution Home Page

http://www.dell.homestead.com/revwar/files/index.htm

The American Revolution Home Page is a bit slow to fully download, but there's much here that a teacher or student will find useful. There is an interactive timeline designed so that each event on the timeline can be clicked to bring up a full page of related information. Beyond the timeline, there are pages dedicated to over 30 prominent figures or events of the Revolutionary War.

Declaring Independence: Drafting the Documents

http://lcweb.loc.gov/exhibits/declara/declara1.html

From the Library of Congress, this straightforward, no-frills site provides a "Chronology of Events" (June 7, 1776, to January 18, 1977), as well as information about, and digital reproductions of, early drafts of the Declaration of Independence. There is good information here for those interested in researching how these landmark documents took shape. This site is part of the larger Library of Congress Web site.

From Revolution to Reconstruction: The Texts

http://odur.let.rug.nl/~usa/D/index.htm

This page is an omnibus collection of links to primary source documents about democracy and the fight for liberty, including the Magna Carta, an account of the Boston Massacre, the Articles of Confederation, the Constitution, and many other documents. Here you will also find the complete Federalist Papers, Washington's Farewell Address, as well as some contemporary British writings. A very broad roundup of primary source documents. This page is a work in progress, but well worth investigating.

The Betsy Ross Homepage
http://www.ushistory.org/betsy/index.html

Probably the best Web site on the life of Betsy Ross and the flag she sewed. Your students can take an online tour of Betsy's Philadelphia home, learn about Betsy's life (thrice widowed), and learn everything—no exaggeration—about the American flag. The site contains quotes and poems about the flag, a picture gallery of flags, flag trivia, a timeline, frequently asked questions, and even flag etiquette (remember how to fold it?). This site is part of the larger History.org Web site, which promotes historic sites in and around Philadelphia, Pennsylvania.

Phillis Wheatley, Poet and Patriot
http://www.forerunner.com/forerunner/x0214_Phillis_Wheatley.html

Born in Senegal and sold into slavery at age seven, Phillis Wheatley was taken in by an exceptional family and was taught English, Greek, and Latin. Her poems became popular in America and England during the turbulent 1760s and 1770s. The following site complements this one, and together they provide an informed view of Phillis Wheatley, America's first published African-American poet.

Diversity and Phillis Wheatley
http://www.pbs.org/ktca/liberty/chronicle/diversity-phyllisw.html

Phillis Wheatley's poetry in praise of George Washington brought her fame and favor. This site provides some background about the ethnic makeup of America during Wheatley's time, with a brief biography at the end. A collection of Wheatley's works can be found on the Poetry Archives @ eMule.com, at http://www.emule.com/poetry/works.cgi?author=59.

Ask the Curator at Valley Forge: Molly Pitcher
http://www.ushistory.org/valleyforge/youasked/070.htm

This is one of the few resources on the Web with detailed information about the well-known heroine of the Revolution. This question-and-answer page describes how Mary Hayes McCauley came to be called Molly Pitcher, and includes an excerpt from a firsthand account of her tenacity during the Battle of Monmouth. Students can send their own questions to the curator at Valley Forge at the end of the page.

The Story of Molly Pitcher
http://sill-www.army.mil/pao/pamolly.htm

Here is the story of Molly on the battlefield, stepping in to work the big gun after her husband collapsed on the field at Monmouth. In recognition of her bravery, George Washington made her a noncommissioned officer.

 WAR OF 1812

War of 1812—1814

http://members.tripod.com/~war1812

This site offers a very thorough collection of texts examining this conflict, including information about the places and players in the war. Students can also look at the soldiers, weapons, Native Americans drawn into the fray, women during the war, and a "Test Your Knowledge" section. The site also includes links to other Web pages about the War of 1812 and links to groups that perform reenactments of famous battles.

Key Events & Causes: War of 1812

http://home.earthlink.net/~gfeldmeth/chart.1812.html

This handy, printable chart should prove useful as a supplement for any unit of study about the War of 1812. It presents a chronological outline of major events leading up to the conflict, beginning in 1806, when the British seized 1,000 U.S. ships to enforce a blockade against France. Along with a listing of each event, the chart provides information on the date, location, and significance of each action.

INDUSTRIAL REVOLUTION

Industrial Revolution and Immigration on Kids Info

http://www.kidinfo.com/American_History/Industrial_Revolution.html

Here is a great, information-rich resource for educators and students about the Industrial Era and the influx of immigrants it attracted to North America. The many links here include pages about Elias Howe (inventor of the sewing machine), Samuel Morse, and the many innovators who followed them into the next century. There are also sections dedicated to railroads, steamboats, inventors, labor unions, and a huge number of links to immigration sites, including the Ellis Island home page. Take a look.

Age of Industry

http://history.evansville.net/industry.html

This is a sort of "Grand Central Station" of Industrial Age links. The large collection begins with a brief introduction on the revolution's English origins, followed by links with information chronicling how the Age of Industry affected textiles, agriculture, transportation, and many other aspects of nineteenth-century life—on both sides of the Atlantic.

Workers in Nineteenth-Century Britain

http://applebutter.freeservers.com/worker/

Here is a primary source Web site that offers another side of the Industrial Revolution. In 1832, British parliamentarian Michael Sadler held an investigation on the appalling conditions of workers, primarily women and children, in Great Britain's textile factories. The outcry about working conditions led the British government to pass the Act of 1833, limiting the hours of labor for women and children in textile factories.

 # WESTWARD EXPANSION

Trails West on Kid Info

http://www.kidinfo.com/American_History/Pioneers.html

Here's another very large collection of educational links to Web sites covering all aspects of the "opening of the West." From this site, you can jump to informative pages on timelines, Web history units, the Texas war for independence, the Oregon Trail, the Mormon Trail, and many links about the California Gold Rush. There are also many pages about famous individuals, ranging from Daniel Boone to Annie Oakley to Chief Sitting Bull. The end of the page contains some "Did You Know..." trivia for students.

The American West

http://www.americanwest.com

A great, in-depth resource of information about the nineteenth-century West, this site includes maps, an extensive section on Native Americans, and areas such as "European Immigration," "Gunslingers and Outlaws," "Pioneer Towns and Forts," "Cowboys," and "Buffalo/Bison." It even has "Western Films," a section depicting images of the old West. There are also links to the Wells Fargo Museum and the National Park Service Web site.

The Oregon Trail

http://www.isu.edu/~trinmich/Oregontrail.html

This is a fun-to-use site with all sorts of good "info-bits" and trivia about the Oregon Trail. "All About the Trail" provides a primer about the historic trail and the westward expansion, while "Fantastic Facts About the Oregon Trail" provides funny-but-true anecdotes of strange events that happened to travelers en route. There's a section of Web links that provide information about places on the trail. Teachers and parents can purchase materials about the trail via this Web site.

California National Historical Trail Wagon Train

http://www.californiawagontrail.com/index.htm

This site follows the fortunes of a group of modern-day pioneers, traveling in covered wagon, on horseback, and on foot from St. Joseph, Missouri, to Sacramento, California, in the summer of 1999. The California Gold Rush Wagon Train was undertaken to honor the 150th anniversary of the original trek of the 49ers through the perils of the unknown. There are diary entries, Q&As, history, maps, a schedule, and paintings created by group members as they made their way through Wyoming, then Idaho and beyond until they reached the Golden State.

The Gold Rush
http://www.pbs.org/goldrush/

Designed around the PBS documentary of the same name, The Gold Rush has a number of useful resources, including "About the Gold Rush," which surveys the discovery of gold in California, the journey west, how people of different cultures and backgrounds created "the ultimate melting pot," and more. A "Fun Facts" section should interest students; the "Classroom Resources" section includes activities, related reading, and links.

The Cherokee "Trail of Tears" 1838–1839
http://rosecity.net/tears/

Another movement west, via dislocation and coercion, was the tragic Trail of Tears, the forced eviction of Cherokee people to Oklahoma from their traditional homelands in Georgia. This site offers a timeline, maps, and a section called "Stories Along the Trail of Tears," which includes articles and letters chronicling this painful chapter of American history.

Trail of Tears
http://www.ngeorgia.com/history/nghisttt.shtml

This informative site surveys the history and fate of the Cherokees of western Georgia, who lived peacefully on their land until the 1830s. Students can find descriptions of the legal battles, forced removal, and hard journey of the Cherokees. Particularly touching is "The Legend of the Cherokee Rose," about the white blossom that is now the official flower of the state of Georgia.

SLAVERY AND THE PASSAGE TO FREEDOM

The Road to Freedom: Using the WWW to Teach About Slavery
http://education-world.com/a_lesson/lesson101.shtml

From the award-winning Education World Web site, this wonderful section provides virtually everything you'll need to teach your students about this area of U.S. history. There are classroom activity ideas, links to slavery teaching resources, lesson plans, anthologies of slave narratives, illustrations, and additional links to related articles. Very extensive and very good.

The Underground Railroad @ nationalgeographic.com

http://www.nationalgeographic.com/features/99/railroad/

A mysterious, dark home page and the sound of a distant train approaching evoke the sense of danger and secrecy of the Underground Railroad. A click on the home page launches this well-made site from National Geographic. In the first section, "The Journey," students imagine that they are slaves who may have an opportunity to escape to freedom. They are asked to choose whether to stay put or try to flee, and that choice determines their path through the site. Once in "The Journey," users can move around to other sections, including "Routes to Freedom," "Classroom Ideas" (grouped by grades), "Resources and Links," and more.

The Underground Railroad

http://education.ucdavis.edu/NEW/STC/lesson/socstud/railroad/contents.htm

The Underground Railroad offers a solid collection of resources to help your students better understand the people and events of the time. This site includes facts about the Underground Railroad, the Abolitionist Movement, the Fugitive Slave Bill of 1850, and a collection of personal narratives, including those of Frederick Douglass and Harriet Tubman. Further, there are selections here from *Uncle Tom's Cabin* and the writings of Walt Whitman. Maps, a bibliography, and links to other resources are included.

Frederick Douglass Papers

http://www.iupui.edu/~douglass/page10.html

This useful page will connect you to a number of Douglass's well-known texts online, including *My Bondage and My Freedom*, as well as links to first-person slave narratives, other Abolitionist materials, and more resources for teachers. This page is from the larger Frederick Douglass Papers project Web site at Indiana University.

S.T.O.P. Homepage

http://www.anti-slavery.org/stop/

Today's students may be surprised to learn that slavery still exists in parts of Africa and Asia—as were the students at a Denver elementary school, who decided to do something about it. The class of fifth graders began a public awareness campaign and helped raise over $70,000 to buy back the freedom of over 2,000 slaves in the Sudan. Their efforts, as well as information on how your class can get involved, can be seen on this Web site, S.T.O.P. Slavery That Oppresses People. The site is linked to the larger American Anti-Slavery Group Web site, at http://www.anti-slavery.org.

 CIVIL WAR

Abraham Lincoln: An Educational Site

http://www.geocities.com/SunsetStrip/Venue/5217/lincoln.html

Here's the place to look if you want a very thorough and fun-to-use site for students learning about Lincoln. This site, created by a history teacher, includes a Civil War timeline, a map, and photos of Lincoln. Information about Lincoln's family is also included, along with texts of Lincoln's most famous speeches, Lincoln facts, and links to other sites.

Links to Lincoln on the Web!

http://www.education-world.com/a_lesson/lesson098.shtml

Here is a rich resource for teachers, with lesson plan ideas about Lincoln and his time keyed to selected Web sites. There are also activities for several grade ranges, as well as links to research sites and related nineteenth-century sites.

The American Civil War Homepage

http://sunsite.utk.edu/civil-war.index.html

This is probably the mother of all Civil War pages, with links to sites covering every possible angle of the Civil War. Not only are there links to sites about Lincoln, secession, major battles, and commanders, but also to pages where you can read about and hear popular music of the time and read letters written by soldiers in the field. Students can also link to sites with information about African-American troops in the war, the role of women, Jewish-American soldiers, and Confederate society and its leaders. There are many primary source documents available through this site, too.

Lesson Plan: The Civil War

http://www.smplanet.com/civilwar/civilwar.html

Extensive Civil War lesson plan material, including recommended books, ideas for integrating reading and writing, enrichment activities, follow-up activities, information about publishing on the Web, and links to other Civil War sites are some of the features of this site.

Links to Sites About the Civil War From Kid Info

http://www.kidinfo.com/American_History/Civil_War.html

Here's another gift to teachers and students from Kid Info, offering a wonderful collection of links about the Civil War and its time in history. This site offers links about the Civil War, historical background sites, photographs, important battles, declarations of secession, slavery, historical documents, and a section of links to biographies of famous individuals of the era.

Civil War Women

http://scriptorium.lib.duke/collections/civil-war-women.html

On this site you can find interesting information about a number of prominent women in Civil War America, including two who were spies (Union and Confederate). Handwritten correspondence has been scanned in so the original letters can be viewed, along with typed transcriptions of the texts. There are also a number of links to other resources on women in the Civil War, as well as a handful of general Civil War links.

 IMMIGRATION

Immigration: Coming to America (with Teacher's Guide)

http://teacher.scholastic.com/immigrat/index.htm

Designed for grades 2–8, this is a big, wonderful site about immigration to the United States, with testimonies and images of young immigrants of yesterday and today. The site offers an interactive tour of Ellis Island, stories about youthful immigrants in the 1920s and 1990s, an oral history scrapbook, and a comprehensive "Teacher's Guide" with lesson-planning suggestions, extensions, assessment, resources, and Web links.

Ellis Island Photos

http://lcweb.loc.gov/rr/print/070_immi.html

Students can view photos of scenes of immigrants arriving at Ellis Island at this Library of Congress site. Downloading the photos takes a bit of time, but students will find them fascinating and informative.

 TURN OF THE CENTURY

Central Pacific Railroad Photographic History Museum

http://cprr.org

Although this home page takes a while to download, it offers a rich visual history of the building of the transcontinental railroad. The first image that appears is the only existing photograph of a joining of the rails connecting the Central Pacific and Union Pacific railroads. Besides historic photos, the site has reproductions of "stereograph" images and links to reproductions of newspaper articles and other documents of the time. (If you click to read one of these accounts, you are presented with a page that looks like a search engine, but the page you selected is already keyed in—just click through to access the page.) Information about Chinese immigrant workers has also been included.

The World of 1898: The Spanish-American War

http://lcweb.loc.gov/rr/hispanic/1898/

From the Library of Congress Web site, this area provides a panorama of the people, places, and events of this complicated conflict involving Spain, Cuba, Puerto Rico, and the Philippines (each of these areas has its own section). Maps, photos, personal narratives, and manuscripts are all here, as well as information on major and minor figures in the Spanish-American War. Of value, too, are pages of information on events such as the abolition of slavery in Puerto Rico, Congressional acts affecting the war, the role of Theodore Roosevelt, and much more.

Theodore Roosevelt: His Life and Times on Film

http://memory.loc.gov/ammem/trfhtml/trfhome.html

This site, from the Library of Congress' American Memory collection, offers digitized film and audio clips of the first president who recognized the power of the newest media— radio and film. If you have a relatively new Pentium or Macintosh with a 28.8 modem (or faster), or know someone who does, you can view digitized versions of some of the early films made of Teddy Roosevelt by Edison's studios. Even if you cannot run these films, there are excellent voice clips of Roosevelt's speeches, a timeline of his life, and an essay. (There are several "media players" available via the World Wide Web, free to individuals, such as RealPlayer™ and RealMedia™, that will allow you to hear and/or see Teddy speak.) For those who prefer a simple, informative overview of Roosevelt's life, you can find it at http://lcweb.loc.gov/rr/histpanic/1898/roosevelt.html.

Gilded Age Documents

http://www.wm.edu/~srnels/giltext.html

A collection of texts presented by William and Mary College, written in the period known as "The Gilded Age," covering roughly the mid-1860s through the early 1900s. There are writings here from a wide range of authors, from Louisa May Alcott and Frank L. Baum to Jack London, Karl Marx, and President Grover Cleveland. Particularly touching is the diary of a Native American girl sent to a missionary boarding school, *The School Days of an Indian Girl* by Zitkala-Sa, an account appropriate for sixth graders and above.

WORLD WAR I AND THE DEPRESSION

World War I—Trenches on the Web

http://www.worldwar1.com

This huge site, dedicated to the Great War and the people and battles that helped shape this "war to end all wars" is probably the most extensive WWI resource on the Web. Features include a solid "Reference Library" (with many topics), site tours, "WWI U.S. Poster Reproductions," a "Book Search," and a "WWI Discussion Forum." The opening page has a "Diplomatic Teletype" banner, featuring digital "telegrams" between Czar Nicholas and Kaiser Wilhelm on the eve of war.

The 1920s

http://www.louisville.edu/~kprayb01/1920s

A labor of love, this omnibus site provides a wealth of resources to inform users about the fascinating 1920s. A visitor can choose among several pathways: A "20s Timeline" (with hotlinks), "People & Trends," and "A Remarkable Decade." Clicking on "People & Trends," for example, will lead to more sections including "The Arts," "News & Politics," "Science & Humanities," "Business & Industry," "Society & Fads," and "Sports." While there are no lesson plans per se here, the site is packed with a lot of good material about this special American decade.

Celebrate the Century: Search the Web for U.S. History of the 1930s

http://www.education-world.com/a_lesson/lesson079.shtml

This site is an interesting way to explore history. It presents a set of commemorative stamps printed by the U.S. Postal Service, which highlight people and events of the 1930s. After a brief introduction about the various stamps, students are asked find answers to questions inspired by images on them, and are then led to Web sites where the answers can be found. Topics range from FDR and the Depression to the invention of *Monopoly*™, the board game.

Webquest: The Great Depression

http://www.plainfield.k12.in.us/hschool/webq1/webquest.htm

A hands-on lesson designed to give your students an idea about life during the Depression. Students are assigned a profession, and then, assisted by online charts and other materials, they are asked to determine what their families could (and couldn't) afford based on their wages. Further, they are asked to calculate how long they would have to save in order to purchase certain items. Students are asked to write essays, do Web research, and other information-gathering work in order to complete various tasks. This site can be paired with We Made Do, a student-created chronicle of the 1930s, at: http://www.mcsc.k12.in.us/mhs/social/madedo/#anchor109615/. This Web project is a work-in-progress from students in Mooresville, Indiana. It focuses on the

1930s—the Great Depression—and includes oral histories from local residents, period photographs, and e-mailed contributions from other witnesses to the era. The students researched prices from the local Mooresville newspaper during the early 1930s, including food, clothing, furniture, and appliances. This page is a good model for an inquiry-based study of this period.

New Deal Network

http://newdeal.feri.org

This educational resource about the New Deal includes "Classroom Resources," a section of additional online resources about FDR and the Depression, links to the National Archives collection of over 4,000 images, and an extensive "Document Library." Special features include "TVA: Electricity for All," and "Been Here So Long," a collection of firsthand narratives by former slaves compiled by federally funded writers as part of the Works Progress Administration (WPA). A worthwhile place to visit.

The New Deal

http://www.davison.k12.mi.us/academic/hewitt9.htm

This simply designed site, using a grid on the home page, provides easy access to an array of resources about FDR, Eleanor Roosevelt, and various New Deal Programs. It also includes "Voices of the New Deal," oral histories collected under the WPA and other programs. This student-generated site includes a biography and links to more information about FDR and the New Deal.

WORLD WAR II AND THE 1940s

What Did You Do in the War, Grandma?

http://www.stg.brown.edu/projects/WWII_Women/tocCS.html

This student-created site is an oral history of Rhode Island women during the Second World War. The main feature of this site is a collection of over 20 firsthand accounts, recorded by students, of life in wartime America. The site offers an introduction, an article about teaching English using oral histories, along with informative essays, a glossary, a timeline, and links to other WWII sites.

North Platte Canteen, North Platte, Nebraska

http://members.tripod.com/~MartinS/

Here is a loving memorial to nostalgia and wartime culture: the story of the North Platte Canteen, where soldiers traveling through the nation's heartland stopped for coffee and conversation. Through stories and photos, the viewer gets a picture of the people, places, and sentiment of the times. A bibliography, as well as related resources and links, are offered on the site. This is a good resource that helps capture the "flavor" of the era.

Women's Land Army

http://arcweb.sos.state.or/us/osu/osuwla.html

During WWII, the U.S. Emergency Farm Labor Service created the Women's Land Army, recruiting women on the home front into brigades to farm and harvest fields in the absence of male farm hands. Teachers (who were available in the summer), homemakers, and women from all walks of life were part of the corps, farming during the day and returning to their homes at day's end. This is not a large site, but it contains many interesting 1940s photographs of the women who were involved in this national effort.

Asian Americans and U.S-Asia Relations: Japanese American Internment

http://www.askasia.org/for_educators/instructional_resources/lesson_plans/asamww2/japint.htm

This is a multi-faceted lesson designed to give students a feeling for the experience of Japanese American citizens who were interned during WWII. Students are given writing exercises, discussion questions, a simulation, and other activities to help them comprehend the experience. Students are asked, for example, what items they would pack if they were forced to leave their homes, not knowing when they would return. Most of the lesson materials are provided via Web links, including a copy of Civilian Exclusion Order No. 5, which mandated the forced evacuation of Japanese Americans from San Francisco.

Japanese American Internment of the Santa Clara Valley

http://scuish.scu.edu/SCU/Programs/Diversity/exhibit1.html

From the Japanese American Resource Center, this online exhibit provides good information and supporting visuals—maps, exclusion orders, a horse stable being revamped as temporary housing for evacuees, and a signed apology by President George Bush. There are links to Internet exhibits depicting several other internment camps, including Crystal City, Texas, and Tule Lake, California. This site is very slow to download, but contains excellent images and facts.

Celebrate the Century: Search the Web for U.S. History of the 1940s

http://www.education-world.com/a_lesson137.shtml

This page challenges students to a Web scavenger hunt designed around commemorative postal stamps that mark the milestones of the decade. Students can view reproductions of U.S. postal stamps related to WWII, Jackie Robinson, the development of antibiotics, the Big Band sound, and other events that helped define the 1940s. Alongside each stamp is a question related to the people or thing depicted; the answer is found by clicking and exploring a Web link provided for the hunt. This is a fun activity that supports teaching about this pivotal decade.

World War II: Guide From the Access Indiana Teaching & Learning Center

http://tlc.ai.org/wwii.htm

Here is a broad collection of Web links to help teachers gather materials for teaching about WWII. It's all here, from "Tuskegee Airmen" to "Japanese Surrender Documents," excerpts from Edward R. Murrow's famous dispatches, and listings of where to find literature for children. Text and audio clips of various news reports are accessible from this site, as well as photo archives, maps, transcripts of famous speeches, and lesson plans offered by grade levels. Jump in and expect to spend some time going through the wealth of materials provided here.

WWII Commemoration

http://gi.grolier.com/wwii/wwii_mainpage.html

From Grolier Online, this is a good informative site about World War II—its causes, major figures, photographs, a "history test," and more. Articles from the *Encyclopedia Americana* provide an overview of the war, along with biographies and articles about key concepts and people. Best for seventh grade and older.

Teaching With Documents: "A Date Which Will Live in Infamy"

http://www.nara.gov/education/teaching/fdr/infamy.html

"A Date Which Will Live in Infamy" is a lesson plan from the National Archives and Records Administration (NARA) with a different approach. The main page provides background on how Roosevelt's famous Declaration of War was written, and from there students can view earlier handwritten versions (via the Web), and see where important revisions were made. Students can, in effect, deconstruct this renowned speech and analyze FDR's choice of words and their context. Students are provided with an analysis worksheet that is printable from the Web, as well as sound clips of FDR giving the speech. There are additional related activities, including writing, class discussion ideas, and interview tips for collecting oral histories.

Powers of Persuasion—Poster Art of World War II

http://www.nara.gov/education/teaching/posters/poster.html

Another interesting online lesson plan from NARA, looking at some of the more striking American propaganda posters of WWII. Students link to the online exhibit Powers of Persuasion: Poster Art of World War II, at http://www.nara.gov/exhall/powers/power.html, and are asked to compare and contrast the posters and to create WWII posters of their own. This lesson plan correlates to several National History Standards as well as one of the standards for Civics and Government.

 HOLOCAUST

Guidelines for Teaching About the Holocaust

http://www.ushmm.org/education/guidelines.html

From the United States Holocaust Memorial Museum, this is a comprehensive set of guidelines for teachers looking at the rationale for bringing this subject into the classroom. It provides in-depth sections like "Methodological Considerations," "Incorporating a Study of the Holocaust Into Existing Courses," and more. A visit to this site is essential as preparation for teaching about this dark chapter in history.

We Remember Anne Frank

http://teacher.scholastic.com/frank/index.htm

A thoughtful, well-rounded Web experience on the life of Anne Frank, her family, and her times is presented at this site. Along with information and texts from the diary, there are interviews with Miep Gies, the woman who hid the Franks in Amsterdam, and Hanneli Pick-Goslar, a childhood friend of Anne's before the Holocaust. There is a very thorough "Teacher's Guide" (grades 3–8) on the site, with a wide range of good activities for your classroom. Lessons are correlated to the teaching standards published by the National Council for the Social Studies (NCSS).

A Teacher's Guide to the Holocaust

http://fcit.coedu.usf.edu/Holocaust

Here is a thorough yet uncomplicated handbook for teaching about the Holocaust. From the home page you can access a timeline, "Teacher Resources," "Student Activities," and information about people and the arts. The "Teacher Resources" page, at http://fcit.coedu.usf.edu/Holocaust/resource/resource.htm provides access to a range of articles, a bibliography (for students and teachers), images, a glossary, a list of museums, and even relevant software to help you teach.

The Diary of Anne Frank

http://www.sis.port.ac.uk/~Kingtr/cal97/sb/annfsource.htm

This is an engaging Web-based tour of Anne Frank's life, with brief surveys of the world outside the hidden annex and the world within. The site, recommended by its authors for ages 9–16, is a good companion for classes reading the book. The site is divided according to three main themes: "Persecution of the Jews," "Into the Annexe," and "Conclusion." Audio clips of diary readings, printable texts from the diary, a section on history, a quiz, and other related activities are all included. This site is from the United Kingdom, so you will find British spellings.

THE 1950s and 1960s

CNN—Cold War

http://www.cnn.com/SPECIALS/cold.war/

From the Cable News Network (CNN), here is a useful resource about the Cold War and the world events that fed and supported it. There are sections on history, culture, technology, espionage, and the development of the atomic bomb. Although this site was designed as a companion to the CNN documentary series of the same name, teachers who haven't viewed the series will nonetheless find a lot of good material in the "Knowledge Bank" section (accessible from the home page), including images, historical documents, interactive maps, a chronology, and profiles of "Cold Warriors." To help you begin, look at Broad Themes of the Cold War, at http://turnerlearning.com/cnn/coldwar/cs_thmes.html.

The Access Indiana Teaching & Learning Center: Korea and the Korean War

http://tlc.ai.org/korea.htm

If you were wondering where to find resources for teaching about the Korean War, look no further. This extensive group of informative links offers access to a broad range of documents, viewpoints, histories, and chronicles of this war. There are also links to lessons, general resources about contemporary Korea, and a series of maps.

The History Place: Protection From the Atomic Bomb

http://www.historyplace.com/specials/abomb/index.html

Here you'll find a simple reproduction of a pamphlet issued by the commonwealth of Massachusetts in 1950 for distribution to the public. This instructional tract, with drawings ("What to do during an A-bomb attack") contains only a few pages but speaks volumes about the Cold War and fears of atomic attack.

The 1900s—The Sixth Decade: 1950–1959

http://members.tripod.com/archer2000/1950.html

A no-nonsense historical timeline of the 1950s, interspersed with links that lead to more information about various events. For a cultural view of the decade, you can visit The Fifties—A Brief History, at http://www.joesherlock.com/fifties11.html. Here your students can learn about cars with tailfins, Levittown housing, the beginnings of McDonalds, the first electric guitar, and much more. Also of interest: 1950s Photo Scrapbook, a black-and-white sentimental journey, found at http://www.joesherlock.com/fifties9.html.

The Access Indiana Teaching & Learning Center: Television

http://tlc.ai.org/televisi.htm

A collection of links to help teachers assemble information about the beginnings of television, its "golden age" in the 1950s, and today's cable networks. There are also links to guides about TV's inventor, Philo T. Farnsworth, and others who helped make it a household item. A virtual exhibit of early televisions, including some imaginative models from the 1950s, can be found at the MZTV Virtual Gallery, at http://www.com/mech1.html.

NASA Apollo 11 30th Anniversary

http://www.hq.nasa.gov/office/pao/History/ap11ann/eagle.html

The home page of this commemorative site opens with a neat animation of the Apollo 11 moon landing, then the viewer is automatically transferred onto the introduction page. To honor the first manned moon landing, NASA has assembled this educational site that includes "Astronaut Comments," "Bibliographies," "Documents," "Galleries," "Timelines," and more. Links to other NASA-related sites.

Vietnam: Yesterday and Today

http://www.oakton.edu/~wittman/

This voluminous site holds an incredible collection of resources about the Vietnam War, as well as information about Vietnam today. Sections include "Tips for Students," "The Vietnam War Chronology," "Teaching the War," "Women," "Vietnamese Perspective," and much, much more. Another good teaching resource about the Vietnam conflict is The Wars for Vietnam, which can be found at http://students.vassar.edu/~vietnam/. This site also gives a good overview of the war, with access to important documents and other Vietnam-related links.

AskAsia: Vietnam

http://www.askasia.org

At the Asia Society's AskAsia Web site you will find two very different but informative units about Vietnam. To focus on the Vietnam War only, visit Vietnam: A Teacher's Guide, at http://www.askasia.org/frclasrm/readings/r000189.htm. Here you'll find a good history of the war, approached chronologically, with activities for study and classroom discussion at the end. For a lesson about post-war reconciliation, Vietnam Challenge chronicles the return of U.S. Vietnam veterans to Vietnam for a goodwill sporting event (go to AskAsia and click Vietnam Challenge icon). This site contains curriculum guides for the elementary, middle, and high school levels, as well as information about present-day Vietnam and the Vietnamese language.

John F. Kennedy—A History

http://members.tripod.com/gbrannen/index.html

This informative site covers the presidential years of John F. Kennedy, the youngest person ever elected to hold that office. The site presents the texts and transcripts of some of JFK's most brilliant moments, including the declaration of his candidacy for President and the first Kennedy-Nixon debates. A photographic chronology of JFK can be found at The History Place—JFK Photo History, at http://www.historyplace.com/kennedy/gallery.htm. Here are images of Kennedy as a boy, naval officer, candidate, and President.

Looking at the 1960s via Rock n' Roll

http://teachers.net/lessons/posts/267.html

This lesson requires a bit of preparation beforehand, but it will help provide students with a window into the youth culture of the 1960s. The activities integrate history and '60s rock 'n' roll, with research into music, civil rights, cultural attitudes, politics, lifestyle, and more. Students read a biography of Martin Luther King Jr., create a timeline (1964–1968), give oral presentations, have group discussions about song lyrics, and create posters and other artwork. Extension activities include learning about the women's movement in the '60s.

WOMEN'S HISTORY

Women's History: Projects on Women Who Changed History

http://teacher.scholastic.com.lessonrepro/lessonplanswomenhist.htm

From Amelia Earhart to Sandra Day O'Connor, this useful site from Scholastic provides a wealth of ideas about teaching women's history. There are projects based on the lives of remarkable women, a collection of essential resources ("Important Dates in U.S. Women's History"), lesson plans (delineated by grade levels), a bank of profiles of distinguished women, and even classroom plays to try out. Take a look!

The National Women's Hall of Fame

http://www.greatwomen.org

Great women deserve their own hall of fame, and here it is, in a digital format. Students can "tour" the hall by clicking on biographies of women inductees, read about women's history (and, in particular, the First Women's Rights Convention in Seneca Falls, New York), and visit "The Learning Center" at http://www.greatwomen.org/lcclrmid.htm. This page has an extensive list of classroom ideas for K–6 and 7–12, as well a section for further sources.

National Women's History Project

http://nwhp.org/month.html

This site is dedicated to teaching and learning about Women's History Month, with many resources, links to women's history organizations, a quiz, and a section of "Ideas to Use" in the classroom. There is an online catalog for ordering materials.

The Featured Document: The Nineteenth Amendment

http://www.nara.gov/exhall/charters/constitution/19th/19th.html

Here is a short, concise synopsis of how the Nineteenth Amendment, which gave women the right to vote, came into being. The original print of the amendment is reproduced here, as well as two photos from the suffragist era.

Political Culture and Imagery of American Women's Suffrage

http://www.nmwh.org/exhibits/suffr_intro.html

From the National Museum of Women's History, this Web-based exhibit allows the user to take a journey thorough the history of women's suffrage, a 72-year struggle from the first proposed amendment to its final passage. An image gallery, a timeline, a quiz, and additional resources are available.

 # CIVIL RIGHTS

My Story: Rosa Parks

http://teacher.scholastic.com/rosa/index.htm

Scholastic presents a well-rounded Web resource, with a great deal of information about the courageous woman who stood at "ground zero" of the Civil Rights movement. Your students will be able to learn about Rosa Park's life, read an interview with her, see images from the struggle, and access a glossary of terms. For teachers, there is an extensive guide with directions on how to use the contents of the site and ideas for research projects, classroom discussions, and more. Correlated to the NCSS teaching standards.

Martin Luther King, Jr.

http://www.seattletimes.com/mlk/index.html

Here you'll find a cleanly designed Web panorama of Martin Luther King's life and work. Areas of this site include "The Man," "The Movement," "The Legacy," "The Holiday," and "Electronic Classroom." The materials in "Electronic Classroom" include student reflections on the legacy of MLK, an interactive quiz, a study guide (with resources for teachers and students), and a section of Internet links.

Little Rock 9, Integration 0?

http://www.kn.pacbell.com/wired/BHM/little_rock/home.html

This classroom-created WebQuest is designed to encourage critical thinking while taking a close look at school integration in history—and in your own cafeteria today. Suggested activities include role-playing and working out a group solution. A teacher's guide includes tips on working with the material, and there are links to other black history and WebQuest sites. (You may want to pair this site with the Brown vs. the Board of Education Web site that follows.)

Brown vs. the Board of Education

http://www.geocities.com/Athens/Olympus/3515/brown.html

Here is a straightforward telling of the famous Topeka, Kansas, case that turned the tide on "separate but equal" schooling for African Americans. Text and pictures are interwoven on this site, helping to evoke the people, places, and atmosphere of the time.

Timeline of the Civil Rights Movement

http://www.wmich.edu/politics/mlk/

A helpful resource for providing an overview of the Civil Rights Movement, this site lets your students review historic milestones from 1954 through 1965, from Brown vs. Board of Education to the March on Washington and Selma. Clicking on the timeline will bring up a window of information and images pertaining to each event.

Martin Luther King Jr. Day on the Net

http://www.holidays.net/mlk/

For the younger set, this upbeat site provides colorful graphics and understandable readings about the lives of Dr. Martin Luther King and Rosa Parks, and information about MLK Day. The text of the famous "I Have a Dream" speech is also available through this site.

The Martin Luther King, Jr. Papers Project

http://www.stanford.edu/group/king

This scholarly resource is a wonderful place to find primary documents on Martin Luther King, including transcripts of speeches, letters, and published articles, as well as biographical information, a chronology, and more. A very large site, it requires a one-time free registration.

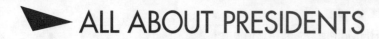

► ALL ABOUT PRESIDENTS

The White House for Kids
http://www.whitehouse.gov/WH/kids/html/kidshome.html

This is a nice way for children, especially those in upper elementary grades, to learn about the history of the White House, the presidency, and the architecture of the White House, today and yesterday. In the first section, "The White House," animated Socks and Buddy (presidential cat and dog) guide students through information on history and the Presidents, pets, and children who have lived at the White House. An online newsletter discusses White House events and the people involved, while other sections include images of special areas of the White House.

American Presidents: Life Portraits
http://www.americanpresidents.org/classroom/

This site, created in partnership with C-SPAN in the Classroom, surveys the lives of our American Presidents, and provides access to teachers guides, a collection of archived student projects, a scavenger hunt, and a test-your-knowledge feature. Individual presidential portraits include personal information (marriage, education, number of children), as well as public service, with data about key events in each administration. From here, you can link to C-SPAN in the Classroom, at http://www.c-span.org/classroom/, where you'll find lesson plans, teaching ideas, and a guide to C-SPAN programming.

The Presidents of the United States of America
http://www.whitehouse.gov/WH/glimpse/presidents/html/presidents.html

The official White House site for biographical summaries of all the U.S. Presidents, arranged chronologically from George Washington to the present day. There is at least one image of each President, links to inaugural addresses, as well as links to information on presidential spouses. This information is kept on the companion Web site, First Ladies of the United States of America, at http://www.whitehouse.gov/WH/glimpse/firstladies/html/firstladies.html. Along with information about each first lady, the home page links to the National First Ladies' Library in Canton, Ohio.

Civics & Government: Resources
http://teacher.scholastic.com/researchtools/articlearchives/civics/resource.htm#living

This site provides a lot of information about the presidency, with a focus on living Presidents. There is a good deal of information here about the workings of government, but the first part of the site is mainly about contemporary Presidents and first ladies, providing many useful resources.

Constitutional Grounds for Presidential Impeachment
http://www.cftech.com/BrainBank/SPECIALREPORTS/impeachment.html

For teachers and researchers, this lengthy treatise on impeachment should provide all the background you need on the subject—from its historical origins and the intent of the framers, to examples of past impeachment inquiries. Very scholarly in its approach, it delves deeply into this important subject.

 # CIVICS AND GOVERNMENT

Project Vote Smart: Vote Smart Classroom
http://www.vote-smart.org/education/

Part of the larger Project Vote Smart Web site (http://www.vote-smart.org), this section focuses on helping teachers educate their students about the democratic process, voting, and the responsibilities of citizens. There are lessons to help students compare and contrast political candidates and to track the voting record of individual members of Congress and the Senate. The "Suggestions for Teachers" section contains activities contributed by classroom educators. There is also an instructional guide to the U.S. government.

Civics & Government: Resources
http://teacher.scholastic.com/researchtools/articlearchives/civics/resource.htm#living

Here is an easy-to-use list of resources all about the workings of our government, and information about the Presidents (past and present) and first ladies of the U.S. Under the heading "U.S. Government/Democracy," there is a great list of links to data on the three branches of government, constitutional rights, democracy in action, and transcripts of online interviews with Senator Patty Murray (D-WA) and others. At the end of the page is a list of classroom lessons, activities, and projects.

USA Government
http://pittsford.monroe.edu/Schools/Jefferson/GOVERNMENT/GovHome.html

Created by students, this resource combines factual information with kid-friendly graphics, making it a good place to visit if your class is researching how government works. This site is not as big or comprehensive as others listed here, but it introduces key concepts about democracy and citizenship to your students.

We the People...
http://www.civnet.org/resoures/teach/lessplan/student1.htm

From the Civnet Web site, here is a bank of lessons designed to help upper elementary students understand the ideas of representative government, the common welfare, civic virtue, and more.

These lessons are laced with discussion questions about the responsibilities and rights of citizens. A related area of the site, http://www.civnet.org/resources/teach/lessplan/level2a.htm, speaks to middle school students, asking, "Why Do We Need a Government?" and "Who is a Citizen?" The lessons presented here include problem solving, discussion starters, and information for teachers on using and reviewing the lessons.

Decisions, Decisions Online
http://www.teachtsp2.com/ddonline/

Based on Tom Snyder's acclaimed software series "Decisions, Decisions," this Web site helps students develop critical-thinking skills, and engage in research, role-play, and debates on important contemporary issues (e.g., gun control). The "Teacher Instructions" area has a detailed, step-by-step "Walk Through" of how to use the materials offered here. Activities use classroom handouts, which can be printed from the site. Teachers need to register on-site, but registration is free.

MULTICULTURAL RESOURCES

Make a Multicultural Calendar
http://www.eduplace.com/ss/act/calend.html

This lesson plan describes a team-oriented project in which upper elementary or middle school students research the traditions of different cultures. The class is divided into 12 groups, each conducting research into one or more traditions or cultures. The groups conduct research to learn about important holidays and dates in the culture, and together create a multicultural calendar. A list of materials, the procedure, and teaching options are included in the text.

United Nations CyberSchoolBus
http://www.un.org/Pubs/CyberSchoolBus/

Here is a fun site for teachers and students, with up-to-date topics and resources about issues all over the world. Educators will find materials here on the environment, health, land mines, poverty, and the status of women. Student resources include "Quiz Quad" and "Elementary Planet." The "Project Materials" area has several curriculum offers for grades 5–12, including units about human rights, urbanization, the environment, and the United Nations. There is also a "Resource Source" section that includes country profiles, statistics, photographs, and data on global trends.

AskAsia
http://www.askasia.org

AskAsia is a pan-Asian site for K–12 educators and students, created and maintained by the Asia Society. The site offers a great deal of material for teachers in the "For Educators" section, including an "Instructional Materials" area that has lesson plans, readings, and a resource locator database (click on your state for Asia-related resources). The majority of the material on the site is for fifth grade and above, although many of the lessons can be easily adapted for younger or older students. Once on the home page, click on the yellow "new" button to see the newest or most popular features. Of special interest: the illustrated *Ramayana* (from India Book House) and "Vietnam Challenge."

Africa: One Continent, Many Worlds

http://www.nhm.org/africa/main.htm

Students can take a comprehensive look at Africa past and present at this site from the Natural History Museum online. It presents a good deal of cultural information, stories, natural history, classroom ideas, slavery, and the Diaspora. Clicking on the "Classroom Ideas" area launches the teacher into a new section with a menu on the left-hand frame. Topics include "Geography and Culture," "Family Traditions," the "Role of Masks," the "Ecology of African Mammals," and more.

Grandfather's House: For Teachers

http://seattleartmuseum.org/exhibitions/grandfathershouse/lessons/teacherNav.htm

A user-friendly site from the Seattle Art Museum, this is a resource for teachers and students about traditional life in Korea. Materials on the site cover a range of lessons and activities, from writing and saying Korean words, to an interactive game that allows students to rearrange Grandfather's house. In the "For Teacher's section," educators will find a grid that aligns site content with visual art concepts and cultural connections. This is part of the larger site for youngsters about Korea called Explore Korea: A Visit of Grandfather's House.

E-Pals.com Classroom Exchange

www.epals.com

This is a great way to introduce your students to their peers around the world, from Canada to Japan to New Zealand. Classrooms can seek out other classrooms from specific grades and locations, with over 100 countries to choose from! There is also an online chat, and teachers can view a sampling of correspondence from e-pals around the world.

Part

3

Language Arts and Literature

▶ GENERAL RESOURCES

Language Arts Standards
http://www.ncte.org/

You can view the National Council for Teachers of English National Standards when you visit this site.

Carol Hurst's Children's Literature Site
http://www.carolhurst.com

This site, considered the premiere site for finding resources about children's literature, has more resources than can be absorbed in one sitting. There are on-site reviews of children's books (accessible by title, author, type, or grade level), curriculum-related books on a wealth of subjects, parenting resources, and a free online newsletter. To begin, click "Expanded Table of Contents" for a feast of resources.

The Children's Literature Web Guide

http://www.acs.ucalgary.ca/~dkbrown/

A straightforward, no-frills collection of resources for teachers, parents, storytellers, writers, and illustrators. There are also links to information in areas such as "Award-Winning Books," "Teaching Ideas for Children's Books," and "Essential Kid Lit Web Sites."

AskERIC Lesson Plans—Language Arts

http://ericir.syr.edu/Virtual/Lessons/Lang_arts/index.html

This useful resource, from the Educational Resources Information Clearinghouse (ERIC) mega-site, has a deceptively simple home page that barely hints at the large number of resources that are just one click away. You'll find teacher-tested language arts lesson plans on literature, journalism, listening, handwriting, reading, spelling, storytelling, and more.

Education World Language Arts Archive

http://www.education-world.com/a_lesson/archives/lang.shtml

From the wonderful Education World site, this language arts archive offers an intelligent array of lesson plans, ranging from teaching writing skills (check "Kids Can W.R.I.T.E.—Write, Revise, Inform, Think, and Edit") to "Every Day Activities in Language Arts." Explore!

Kathy Schrock's Guide for Educators—Literature & Language Arts

http://school.discovery.com/schrockguide/arts/artlit.html

This site includes a long list of language arts Web sites, handpicked by Kathy Schrock for her renowned *Guide for Educators on the Web*. The sites are listed alphabetically, but with this many quality sites on hand, you can't go wrong. No matter what topic you are researching, there's a good chance you'll find something relevant here.

Lesson Plans for Your English Class

http://www.net-language.com

This site offers teachers lesson plans keyed to major stories appearing each day in *The New York Times*. The lesson plans and *NYT* articles are free to download. A lesson plan archive is available on the site as well. A good way to combine language arts and current events in the classroom.

Biography Maker

http://www.bham.wenet.edu/bio/biomak2.htm

Here's a helpful "how-to" site for students learning to write biographies, courtesy of Washington state's Bellingham Public Schools and Jamie McKenzie, publisher of *FromNowOn*, a staff development journal.

CREATIVE WRITING

Young Writer's Clubhouse
http://www.realkids.com/club.shtml

Let your students jump into this kid-friendly Web site, an easy-to-use resource that leads students step-by-step through the writing process. Created by children's author Deborah Morris (*Real Kids, Real Adventures*), the information here is clear and speaks directly to a young audience. Helpful sections include "Keys to Writing Success," a comprehensive guide to getting stories published, and "Young Writer's Critique Group," where kids' writings are shared and evaluated by their peers. There are also opportunities for young authors to enter writing contests via this site. Students can register online to join the Young Writer's Clubhouse free of charge.

KidPub
http://www.kidpub.org/kidpub/

Here's a site completely devoted to publishing children's stories, with featured tales (old and new) by kids, a searchable database of stories, a special area where classroom work is published, a "Story Form" that helps youngsters submit their stories, a detailed "How-To" section on publishing stories, and more. There is also an area where students can find "KeyPals" (Internet penpals) and correspond via e-mail. An award-winning site your students are sure to enjoy.

Young Author's Workshop
http://www.planet.eon.net/~bplaroch/index.html

This site, geared for students in grades 4–7, is designed to help jump-start the creative writing process. Written in a simple and direct style, this resource offers thematically grouped Web links to help students identify ideas and find advice on writing, revising, editing, and publishing. It also includes a "Teacher Resources Page."

Young Writers: Feature Articles
http://www.inkspot.com/joe/young/articles

Part of the well-known Inkspot writer's resource site, this area is tailored for youngsters and teenage writers. Here they will find a series of texts to encourage and inspire creative writing and screenwriting, including "Advice for Young Writers," "Beginning Writer's FAQ (Frequently Asked Questions)," interviews with teenage writers, and "Tips for Aspiring Young Screenwriters" from a writer for the popular kids network, Nickelodeon. Links to the main Inkspot site.

 # POETRY

Poetry Pals, the K–12 Student Poetry Publishing Project

http://www.geocities.com/EnchantedForest/5165/

This site is big—and we mean big—and it is a treasure trove of resources designed to teach and encourage the writing of poetry. This is an international publishing project that integrates learning about various styles of poetry with examples from classrooms around the world. Guidelines for publishing students' poetry are included, as well as an extensive list of lessons and activities. Activities are designed for online as well as offline student research.

Poetry Writing With Jack Prelutsky

http://teacher.scholastic.com/writwit/poetwit/index.htm

Another wonderful free guide from the Scholastic Network can be found in the "Write With..." series. Here is a five-step look at the poetry writing process with well-known children's poet Jack Prelutsky. Tips on managing time, extension activities, and additional resources are available on the site. Students can hear an audio clip of the author reading one of his poems, and take up the "challenge" of composing the rest of a poem that Prelutsky has started online.

Sonnet Central

http://www.sonnets.org

The mother of all sonnet sites, there's nothing left out of this deep knowledge resource. There's a tour of "The Sonnet in Great Britain" (listed by chronological era), and sections for sonnets originating in other countries, including the U.S., Ireland, Australia, and New Zealand. There's an alphabetical listing of authors, a bibliography, an area for submitting sonnets, a timeline, and, of course, a section about writing sonnets. Definitely a worthwhile place to visit.

Haiku

http://www.indiana.edu/~japan/japan/mdnjapan/LS3.html

Designed for upper elementary classrooms (but adaptable to other grades), this lesson helps you teach the art of writing haiku, which originated in Japan but inspires writers everywhere. The activities involve writing haiku in groups and individually, with a number of good examples. There is additional information about tanka poetry, a form consisting of 31 syllables, with an example written by a student.

Listen and Write: Poetry

http://www.bbc.co/uk/education/listenandwrite/index.shtml

From the BBC—of all places—here's a children's site that encourages poetry writing through writing rap lyrics (grades 3–6). Cute graphics introduce students to sections that include "The Rap Realm" (and within that, "What is Rap?," with an exercise in writing a haunted-house rap). "The World of Wonderwords" is hosted by a creature known as The Saurus, helping kids find the words they need. There are online quizzes in each section. If your computer has a fairly recent version Web browser, either Netscape 4 or Microsoft Internet Explorer 4 or later, you can see animations in the "hi-tech" version. RealPlayer™ (downloadable for free) is needed to hear examples of poems.

 # EXPLORING LITERATURE

Folktale Writing—Writing With Writers, From Scholastic Network

http://teacher.com/writewit/folk/index.htm

An exploration of the art of writing folktales, with published storyteller Alma Flor Ada as your guide. The site offers a five-step process for writing and publishing your students' works online. A good "Teachers Guide," linked to this section (grades 2–8), provides data on learning objectives, how to use the project in class, extension activities, resources, assessment tips, and more.

Folklore, Myth, and Legend

http://www.acs.ucalgary.ca/%7Edkbrown/storfolk.html

From the very comprehensive *Children's Literature Web Guide*, this page offers links to a large collection of well-known folktales and myths, from *Aesop's Fables* to old Indian legends. If you can't find or purchase the folktales to support a mythology lesson, many of the classic texts can be found here.

Tales of Wonder—Folk and Fairy Tales From Around the World

http://darsie.ucdavis.edu/tales/

This award-winning site is an easy-to-navigate collection of popular folktales from around the world, including Central Asia, Siberia, Africa, Ireland, the Middle East, and more. A great addition to any lesson in which you want to include a multicultural perspective.

Literary Concepts—Elements of a Story (Outline)

http://lausd.k12.ca.us/~cburleso/Lessons/LiteraryConcepts.htm

A useful classroom handout that lists the basic elements of telling a story, with definitions of terms (irony, character, protagonist, and so on). This site contains links to the larger Los Angeles Unified School District Web site, which contains many helpful resources.

The Access Indiana Teaching and Learning Guide to Judy Blume

http://tlc.ai.org/blumeidx.htm

This site includes a collection of links to help you investigate one of the favorite storytellers of the preteen set. If you want to explore the world of Judy Blume, or check out plot summaries, biographical information, interviews, and more, begin here. There are links to sections of Judy Blume's Home Base, at http://www.judyblume.com .

Mark Twain and His Times

http://etext.lib.virginia.edu/railton/index2.html

America's legendary storyteller has several homes on the Web, but this site, from the University of Virginia, is a great starting point. There are texts, reviews (by Twain's contemporaries), photos, the "Memory Builder Game," a search feature, and more resources than can be listed here. For a more concise overview of Samuel Clemens's career and life as Mark Twain, along with many biographical links, check About.com's section on Twain, at: http://marktwain.about.com/arts/books/marktwain/library/letters/bl_letter_bio.htm .

Book Adventure

http://www.bookadventure.com

Imagine being able to quickly match students with books that are just right for them! That's just what this site does. It includes synopses of those books, a "Quiz-O-Matic" that tests students on what they've read, and redeemable prizes for passing the quiz. This is a site designed to entice kids to read by combining incentives, good books, and zany graphics. By far the most useful tool on this site is the "Book Finder," through which students (K–8) can search for a recommended book to read. Users enter their grade and subject preference (they can also search by author, title, or ISBN number). The site's database searches among its 2,500+ titles, and a printable page appears on-screen with a list of compatible books. Clicking on the book title will bring up a synopsis of the story. Although kids and teachers must register to use Book Adventure, registration is free. This site, produced by the Sylvan Reading Game Foundation, has been developed under an advisory committee that includes the International Reading Association and the National Association of Elementary School Principals.

Read In!

http://www.readin.org

The Read In! is an annual "Internet event" that has been drawing over 300,000 participants in the past few years; a day-long (8:00 A.M.–8:00 P.M.) festival of reading where children can "chat" online with as many as 22 of the most popular children's authors. On the day of the Read In!, kids bring pillows and plenty of books. Classrooms registered for the Read In! (it's free to schools) receive "chat" software at no cost about one month before the actual event. At designated times, the class goes online to discussion areas where your students can meet kids from places like South Dakota and South Africa. Once online, your students exchange information about the books they are reading, discuss classroom activities, recommend books to one another, and "chat" with authors and special guests (all under a teacher's supervision, of course). In 1999, featured authors included Judy Blume, Ed Emberly, R. L. Stine, and many others. There are "practice" online sessions for the novice and transcripts of the day's proceedings available afterwards. The Read In! was founded in 1993 by Jane Coffey, an elementary school teacher from Turlock, California, and former software reviewer for Scholastic's Electronic Learning magazine.

Virtual Narnia

http://members.tripod.com/~AMelashenko/index.html

A nice companion site for young fans of the classic *Chronicles of Narnia* books by C.S. Lewis. Included in this colorful site are games, an encyclopedia of characters, creatures, and places, a timeline, a teacher's bulletin board, and more.

Part

4

Mathematics

 GENERAL RESOURCES

Math Standards

http://www.nctm.org/

The complete listing of the national math standards can be viewed or downloaded at this site.

The Math Forum

http://forum.swarthmore.edu/

One of the very best, this award-winning site is a great first stop for math teachers and students. The Math Forum has a wealth of useful features, including the "Teacher's Place" section and a "Student Center." The teacher's area has valuable information grouped by grade levels, including lesson plans, Internet activities, and reviews of math software. Additionally, the site has goodies such as "Teacher2Teacher" (a math question-and-answer service), Web units contributed by Forum users, a "Problem of the Week" page, as well as links to discussion groups, a math library, and workshop announcements. The "Student Center" offers resources by grade levels, a help area called "Ask Dr. Math," an "Internet Math Hunt," and "Math Tips & Tricks," which includes "BeatCalc," beat-the-calculator game.

This Is MegaMathematics!

http://www.cs.uidaho.edu/~casey931/mega-math/menu.html

This site combines math with fun for primary and middle school grades. It includes topics that range from "The Most Colorful Math of All" to "Algorithms and Ice Cream for Everyone." Each MegaMath topic offers "Activities," "Big Ideas and Key Concepts," "Background Info," "Vocabulary," NCTM Standards Correlations, and other relevant links. MegaMath is a project of the Computer Research Applications Group at Los Alamos National Laboratory.

A+ Math

http://www.aplusmath.com

Another student-friendly math site, A+ Math has a "Game Room," online "Flash Cards," a "Homework Helper," and "Advanced Problems." There are interactive features designed to help students learn math in an engaging way, including a "Concentration" game (multiplication and addition versions), an interactive multiplication table, and fraction inequality flashcards.

AskERIC Lesson Plans—Mathematics

http://ericir.syr.edu/Virtual/Lessons/Mathematics/index.html

This deceptively simple page is the gateway to many lesson plans across a range of topics. Lesson plans include algebra, applied math, whole numbers, addition, subtraction, geometry, process skills, and more. Lessons are also given a recommended grade range.

 THE BASICS

AllMath.com

http://www.allmath.com

A nice all-purpose math site that will help your students review the basic building blocks across topics for the upper primary and early middle school grades. Multiplication tables, flashcards, a metric converter, and reference pages (including "Biographies of Math") are all here, along with a glossary, a help page, "The Magic Square Game," and links to other relevant math sites.

Math-O-Magic

http://tqjunior.advanced.org/5595/Index/index.html

Students wrote much of Math-O-Magic, and kids should feel right at home going through the site. It is designed to help students with addition, subtraction, and multiplication, and it includes story problems and games. For the intrepid math student, there are "Challenge" and "Super Challenge" sections, with more difficult problems that branch out into geometry and other math concepts.

Mrs. Glosser's Math Goodies

http://www.mathgoodies.com/lessons

This collection of math resources was created with grades five through eight in mind, although slightly younger (and older) students may be able to make use of it as well. Subjects offered include "Integers," "Understanding Percent," "Number Theory," "Circumference & Area of Circles," and more. There are also links to math puzzles and a math chat area.

Middle School: A Math Web Site

http://www-personal.umd.umich.edu/~jobrown/math.html

Here is a "best-of" Web page, with a selection of 15 sites designed to help middle school students tackle a variety of mathematical subjects. Each recommended Web site is "hot-linked" for one-click access, and the page includes commentaries and suggestions for extension activities related to each site.

Fast Facts—Math

http://www.mccc.edu/~kelld/page400.html

If you need to review some key concepts before you begin that exercise in cubic measurements —or graphing lines, real numbers, decimals, and a host of other topics—you can find quick relief in the Fast Facts Web site. This very easy-to-use site will promptly connect you with the information you need.

AskERIC Lesson Plans—Mathematics: Arithmetic

http://ericir.syr.edu/Virtual/Lessons/Mathematics/Arithmetic/index.html

A simple list of classroom-tested lesson plans in arithmetic, listed alphabetically by title with a recommended grade level. Lessons include "Learning About Ratios: A Sandwich Study Guide" (grades 4–6), "Mental Mathematics" (grades 4–5), and "Easy Addition" (grades 4–12). There are also lessons here for the early primary grades.

 # MONEY

Moneyopolis!

http://www.moneyopolis.com/main.asp

Welcome to the virtual town of Moneyopolis, where new arrivals receive a make-believe $600 "New Resident's Stake" to help them get started. As town residents, students "tour" seven town centers, including a job center, a shopping center, a community center, city hall, and other institutions. At each center, students are given three math challenge questions. Each correct answer earns $10, plus $50 for the bonus question. The goal: to save $1,000 and earn a minimum of three Community Center Service Medallions. Activities are for classroom use, and the math skills required in the game are correlated to the NCTM standards.

Big Money Adventure
http://www.agedwards.com/bma/index.shtml

The Big Money Adventure offers three levels of play: ages 2–6, 6–10, and 10–adult. To enter the adventure, players choose an on-screen guide that will help them make decisions, with names like "Gold Bullion," "Sell-Hi," and "Pixie Profit" (with personalities to match). The youngest are directed to "Rainbow Castle," where they can play games and print out coloring pages. The next level, "Storybook Adventures," lets kids in the 6–10 group choose the path their characters will travel while they learn about investing. The game for older players, "Star Traders," requires picking five stocks from a preselected list and measuring their performance.

Teaching Money
http://www.atozteacherstuff.com/lessons/money.html

Two lesson plans with step-by-step instructions to help your students learn money values (counting money) are presented here. Designed for fourth-grade students, one of the lessons begins with the students reading a Shel Silverstein poem ("Smart," from *Where the Sidewalk Ends*). The second lesson builds on the first, and students discuss spending money. From the "A to Z Teacher Stuff" Web site.

Classic 164 Currency Converter
http://www.oanda.com/converter/classic

A no-frills, online currency converter that allows an instant view of the exchange rates among 164 currencies around the world. Additionally, you can find the historical exchange rates for the currencies for any date going back to 1990. This site, updated nightly, can be used as a tool for a variety of math or economics exercises, and can be integrated into a social studies lesson as well.

 # GEOMETRY

Geometry Center
http://www.scienceu.com/geometry/

This student-friendly site walks through the basics of shapes, patterns, and symmetry. It includes suggested activities, articles, a "Facts-Figures section," a "Classroom" area, an online library, and an assortment of other places to visit. There is an electronic store for ordering materials accessible through the site.

Geometry

http://tqd.advanced.org/2647/geometry/geometry.htm

"Geometry" is a site designed by students to help their peers navigate through the various aspects of geometry. Learners will find a large glossary, along with pages on constructions, angles and lines, measurement formulas, sample problems, Greek prefixes, and other topics.

Picture This! —Tangrams for Kids

http://www.geocities.com/Eureka/Suite/3789/PAGE4.html

Here's an entry into the world of geometry that combines art and angles for the younger set. Welcome to tangrams, a very old form of puzzle-making originating in China. The art of tangrams begins with seven puzzle pieces, (two large triangles, two small triangles, a medium-sized triangle, a square, and a parallelogram). Kids are asked to make their own tangram picture, and an online gallery of kids' "Tan-scapes" is included. Tangrams are used to teach students geometric spatial relationships and problem solving while sharpening their creativity.

Fractals

http://math.rice.edu/~lanius/frac/

Fractals are geometric figures with special properties. There are sections on making several types of fractals, a "For Teachers" section, and "Fractal Properties" area, including self-similarity, fractional dimensions, and formation by "iteration." This is an award-winning site designed for elementary and middle school use.

Geometry Problem of the Week

http://forum.swarthmore.edu/geopow/

For middle school (and older), this is a great learn-by-example geometry site. Schools and individual students around the country take on the geometry problem of the week (displayed on the first page of the site), then electronically submit their solutions and explanations. Highlighted solutions from students are posted on the site the following week, along with the Web instructor's solution and a new challenge for the coming week. This is another great project from the omnibus Math Forum Web site.

 # REAL WORLD MATHEMATICS

Math in Daily Life

http://www.learner.org/exhibits/dailymath/

Math in Daily Life is the Web site that asks, "How do numbers affect everyday decisions?" The message here for students is that all of us need math for the tasks we do every day, and lessons include math used in cooking, home decorating, metric conversions, and other topics. The site, part of an online Annenberg/CPB Projects Exhibits Collection, offers related resources, as well as access to other Annenberg Exhibits online.

CNBC Student Stock Tournament

http://sst.cnbc.com

This site hosts a twice-yearly tournament for students in fourth grade and above. Student teams (from 3 to 25 students) register on-site and have an imaginary $100,000 to invest. They must assemble a portfolio of stocks currently traded on the major exchanges, tracking the real stock performances for three months. The CNBC cable network broadcasts highlights from those teams whose portfolios show the highest earnings. There are winners announced each week (weekly winners receive T-shirts). At the end of the tournament, CNBC donates 300 shares of General Electric stock to the school with the highest-earning team. There is a "Teachers Only" section that allows teachers to create a "practice portfolio," as well as "Educational Resources," a "Financial Tools" section, and an "Investor's Café."

Math: Real World

http://www.teachnet.com/lesson/math/matrea.html

These lessons from Teachnet.com provide a number of approaches for teaching "real world" math to your class. You can budget a virtual trip to the grocery store, plan a vacation (calculating distances and gas mileage), have your students calculate credit-card interest, and more.

Online Math Applications!

http://tqjunior.advanced.org/4116/

This site is designed to show students where math fits into music, history, investing, science, and travel. Students can play a simulated stock market game, learn about the "Mozart Effect," read about famous mathematicians and learn about PCs. This is also a site developed by students for their peers.

DECIMALS AND FRACTIONS

Teaching Decimals

http://online.edfac.unimelb.edu.au/485129/DecProj/sources/welcome.htm

This comprehensive site for teachers from the University of Melbourne, Australia, focuses on the subject of how to teach decimals. This solid resource offers the basic concepts about decimals, case studies that explore the ways students think about decimals, and a teaching area that provides ideas for lesson plans and tests. The site also allows you to download educational games for your students. An on-site glossary is also available.

A Tour of Fractions

http://forum.swarthmore.edu/paths/fractions

A thematically grouped page of resources, with "Lessons and Materials," "Questions and Answers about Fractions," and recommended software. There are also links to general fraction references for students and more questions and answers from "Ask Dr. Math." Another great resource from the Math Forum Web site.

The Relationship Among Fractions, Decimals, and Percents

http://www.mccc.edu/~kelld/CompFDP.htm

A quick review, written in simple, large print, which presents the basics of converting fractions to decimals, percents to fractions, decimals to fractions, and so on. At the end of the page, you can link to a "Percents Problem Solving" area. This site is part of the Math Online Learning Center.

No Matter What Shape Your Fractions Are In

http://math.rice.edu~lanius/Patterns/

Here's a simple game involving cutout patterns that combines fractions and geometry. Teachers can do these exercises offline with classes. Additionally, if the page is viewed with a Java-enabled Web browser (either Netscape 4.0 or Microsoft Internet Explorer 4.0 or later), the images can be manipulated online. There are links here to four more fraction games and other math lessons.

Mighty M&M Math Experiment

http://mighty-mm-math.caffeinated.org/home.htm

Yes, this game uses one of America's favorite candies to help kids learn percentages. Kids work in teams and figure the percentages of each color. Suggested extension exercises are included (graphing the results, entering the results on a spreadsheet, and so on).

Part

Other Great Sites for Teachers

 ART

KinderArt

http://bconnex.net/~jarea/lessons/

A world of art lessons is one click away. This site has lessons, craft ideas, and thematic units that are mainly K–6, although some can be applied through the eighth grade. A navigation panel on the right side of the screen allows you to view lessons by catgeory: "Cross-Curriculum," "Drama," "Crafty Ideas," "Seasonal," "Sculpture," "Recycling," "Painting," "Textiles," "Multicultural," and more. There is also a section here for the preschool set. Teachers can also contribute lessons to the collection via a special page on the site.

Elementary Art Lessons

http://www.artswire.org/~kenroar/lessons/elem/elemlessons.html

From ArtsWire, the nonprofit group that keeps its finger on the pulse of the art world. Here you'll find a variety of lessons, mostly contributed by teachers. The "Elementary" area holds over 50 lessons and activities, from scratch art to Native American sand painting. The page for older students offers roughly 30 activities, including "Pastel Pointillism!" and "Flowers a la O'Keefe."

Teacher's Guide to American Art

http://www.thinker.org/fam/education/publications/guide-american/index.html

This is a wonderful, in-depth guide from the Fine Arts Museum of San Francisco. Although this site was initially created to prepare students for an exhibit of American art at San Francisco's De Young Museum, this very thorough tour should be useful to teachers anywhere. The guide focuses on works by American artists from colonial times through the 1880s. In addition to looking at artworks online, there are related history lessons to help provide background. "Lesson Plan #1" provides a good lesson in American paintings (click on the small paintings or "slides" to increase their size). Students are taught to distinguish between a portrait, still life, genre, and landscape, and are provided with a glossary of art terms. Lessons are designed for the fifth grade and above.

The @rt Room (The Art Room)

http://www.arts.ufl.edu/art/rt_room/@rtroom_home.html

The @rt Room is a place for children ages 8 and up to explore various aspects of art. Clicking on the "@rtroom Doorway" will lead students to a group of art activities, online exhibitions, facts about famous artists, an art library, and a section called "@rt Sparklers," which encourages kids to "think like an artist." There is also an area where children can find books written by other children, and a section of related links.

Religious Beliefs Made Visual: Geometry in Islam

http://www.askasia.org/frclasrm/lessplan/1000030.htm

Here's a lesson in art as well as multicultural perspectives, in which students learn to construct two geometric patterns common in Islamic art. The lesson includes printable handout sheets for the classroom, as well as a good background essay in Islamic beliefs, and the significance of the infinitely repeating patterns found in this type of art. The lesson, by art educator Jane Norman, is written for teachers, and probably best applied to fifth grade classes and older.

How-To Posters

http://www.eduplace.com/ss/act/howto.html

This is an uncomplicated project combining art and language arts that your students should find engaging. Students discuss, select, and then research some survival skill or craft utilized by colonial settlers or Native Americans—for example, building a canoe, making tools, food-gathering, or making clothes. After doing the research, students (individually or in teams) create how-to posters that describe how to perform the skill or craft. Posters should include step-by-step drawings or diagrams, photocopies of pictures, explanatory texts and labels, and be accompanied by an oral presentation. From Houghton Mifflin's Education Place site.

VIRTUAL TOURS OF AMAZING PLACES

The Franklin Institute Science Museum

http://www.fi.edu

One of the most kid-friendly science museums has one of the most kid-friendly sites on the Web. There are a number of wonderful exhibits on this award-winning site, including "The Heart," "Ben Franklin," "The Universe," and "Undersea and Oversee." Teachers can access online units of study via this site ("Wind" and "Living Things"), as well as a series of classroom activities and an "Educational Hotlist" of recommended Web sites.

The Exploratorium

http://www.exploratorium.org

Another great children's museum that has generated a great Web site. There are a host of super online exhibits here, as well as "The Learning Studio," a special area of recommended exhibits and Web sites. Each month, "The Learning Studio" identifies 10 "Cool Sites" for science, art, or general education; there is also an archive of over 400 previously reviewed sites ("Still Cool"). The "Digital Library" area lets users explore collections of past exhibits and digital images. A must-see!

The Smithsonian

http://www.si.edu/

A big, institutional site holding many digitized collections, online exhibits, links, and other resources. Of particular interest to teachers, Smithsonian Education at http://educate.si.edu offers a series of free lesson plans in the arts, language arts, science, and social studies. These lessons are methodically constructed and link to related resources from the vast trove of Smithsonian online resources.

The Metropolitan Museum of Art: The Glory of Byzantium

http://www.metmuseum.org/htmlfile/Education/byzantium/byzhome.html

This is where the Web can really shine, in presenting rare and precious objects that might otherwise be out of reach for millions of people. A prime example is the Metropolitan's The Glory of Byzantium, an online exhibit and with in-depth educational material. Teachers should look at the "Teacher Resources" page, at http://www.metmuseum.org/htmlfile/Education/byzantium/teach.html, for an introduction to Byzantine art, information about materials, techniques, class activities, and discussion topics. Most of the images presented here are "thumbnails," which means that clicking on these pictures will bring up larger, more detailed images. This section links to the main education page, which includes a "For Kids" section with games, guides, and hunts.

Louvre Museum

http://www.louvre.fr/

The official Web site of the world-famous Louvre can be toured in French, English, Spanish, or Japanese. The stunning visual collections include "Paintings" (with its resident superstar, the Mona Lisa); "Egyptian Antiquaries;" "Greek, Roman, and Etruscan Antiquaries;" "Prints and Drawings;" "Sculpture," and more.

Natural History Museum of Los Angeles

http://www.nhm.org

This modest home page doesn't indicate the wealth of resources offered by this museum. A good place to start is "The Guide to Museums and Cultural Resources (Site Map)," which lists all the online presentations about animals, art and photography, and history and culture. Recommended is the "Africa: One Continent, Many Worlds" area, which is very rich in educational resources.

Carnegie Museum of Natural History

http://www.clpgh.org/cmnh/index.html

Pittsburgh's Carnegie Museum of Natural History has a good collection of educational online exhibits, including "China's Feathered Dinosaurs," "North South East West: American Indians and the Natural World," and the award-winning "Life in Ancient Egypt." To tour the online exhibits, begin at the exhibits index page, at http://www.clpgh.org/cmnh/exhibits/online.html.

 # SPANISH

TeachSpanish.com

http://www.teachspanish.com

A Spanish teacher created this useful site for colleagues in the field. There are lesson plans for elementary, middle, and high school classes, links to various sites about individual Spanish-speaking countries, a quick tour of national flags, and a great collection of "Teacher Resource Sites." Other on-site goodies include a link to an international currency conversion engine, a message board, and a page where Spanish teachers can get ideas on how to raise funds for class projects. A handbook for Spanish teachers, *Vamos a Jugar*, is available through the site at a discount price.

Especially Español

http://edweb.sdsu.edu/edfirst/spanish

This well-researched Web site is divided into four sections: a description of "Hotlists," with links to a few Spanish-resource megasites; activities and resources for elementary schools; activities and resources for middle and high school; and links to supporting online resources. The elementary section offers guidance on how to use the recommended resources with your students, and the middle/high school section provides information on sites that should engage your class. There are also links here to help your students find pen pals and build an Internet home page, as well as some general Web-using tips for the teacher.

Electronic Flashcards for Spanish

http://www.emporia.edu/biosci/span/flshcrd.htm

A practical, easy-to-use Web tool that provides a simple way to review the basics. Using frames to split the lower half of the screen, the user clicks on, for example, "Verb Conjugations." On the right side of the screen a list of verbs will appear (in Spanish); by clicking on a particular word, the proper conjugations of the verb appear on the left side of the screen. A tried-and-true way to self-test and reinforce vocabulary. Good for beginners.

Study Spanish

http://www.studyspanish.com

This is a site for beginners in middle school and older. It contains an extensive list of topics (from "Possessive Adjectives" to "Weather Expressions") presented in clear, unambiguous language. Information is presented simply, without fussy graphics, and there are links to on-site exercises, vocabulary, and other options. Users can link to printer-friendly versions of each lesson page, for quick printouts. Further, learners can be notified of new lessons if they choose to enter their e-mail addresses on the site.

Hot Internet Sites en Español!

http://www.pacbell.com/wired/fil/pages/listspanish.html

Part of Pacific Bell's Knowledge Network collection, this site is a good friend to teachers of intermediate Spanish-language students, or students who are fluent speakers. The site provides access to the Alta Vista Web translation service (English-language sites can be viewed in Spanish, and vice versa), Spanish sites for elementary school children, secondary students, and a solid list of teaching resources. A "must" for Spanish or bilingual education teachers.

Mundo Zoo (World Zoo)

http://www.familia.cl/newweb/animales/animal.htm

Here's a fun place for young Spanish-speaking students. Mundo Zoo provides clear color photographs of favorite animals from around the world, including the prehistoric. Students will find descriptions of the animals and learn where they live and how they survive. The site links to other zoo Web sites as well as other animal-related sites.

Vistas Del Sistema Solar (Views of the Solar System)

http://www.hawastsoc.org/solar/span/homepage.htm

This is a beautiful site with gorgeous photos of the planets, the sun, and cosmic phenomena—including comets, asteroids, and meteorites. This Spanish-language resource can be used by middle school students in many ways—as in a cross-disciplinary project combining Spanish language, astronomy, and computer literacy. Links to other online astronomy resources can be accessed from the home page.

National Clearinghouse for Bilingual Education

http://www.ncbe.gwu.edu

This is a vast, all-in-one site for bilingual education teachers. Features of the NCBE site include an online library, a "Bibliographic Database," "Success Stories" (describing effective teaching practices), an "In the Classroom" section that includes schools on the Web (with lesson plans and other materials), a conference calendar, and a "State Resources" area that reviews the language and teaching requirements for each of the 50 states. Additional features include a weekly online news bulletin (NCBE Newsline) and links to other language and education databases.

 # HOW-TO GUIDES AND TOOLS

Harnessing the Power of the Web—Global Schoolhouse

http://www.gsn.org/web/index.htm

If you are just becoming familiar with the online world, and you'd like to take advantage of its vast resources, this Web site is a good place to start. It offers offers sections such as "Internet Project-Based Learning," "Internet Research," "Building a Collaborative Web project," as well a "Library of References, Readings and Resources." In the online library there's a useful guide to HTML, including instructions on building your first home page. This site is part of the larger Global Schoolhouse Web site (http://www.gsn.org), a very popular Web site for educational projects and resources. Take a look!

Understanding and Using the Internet: A Beginners' Guide

http://www.pbs.org/uti/begin.html

A good primer for taking the first steps onto the Net. Visitors to this site, offered by the Public Broadcasting Service (PBS), will find a helpful overview and a guide to commonly used applications, including electronic mail (e-mail), the World Wide Web, file transfer protocol (FTP), and others, as well as resources for creating your own home page.

From Now On: The Educational Technology Journal

http://www.fno.org

Here is a free online magazine with a lot of practical advice on how to teach with technology. There are sections about curriculum, grants, technology planning, and much more, as well as a section where readers can research prior issues. While browsing, you might want to look at "Why in the World Wide Web?," an article that explores the "whys" of launching a school Web site (http://www.fno.org/mar97/why.html). FNO also links to a dedicated staff development Web site, at www.staffdevelop.org.

Road Map to the Web for Educators: Search Engines

http://www.thejournal.com/features/rdmap/hs116n.cfm

Hold on to your keyboard! This comprehensive listing (with brief reviews) of Internet search engines has something for everyone, and will keep you busy for days. Whatever you may be searching for, there's no doubt you'll find it using one of these search engines, many of them education-specific. The first link, Search Engine Watch (http://www.searchenginewatch.com) is a primer on search engines. It explains what they do and how they work, with reports on various popular engines. From *T.H.E. (Technological Horizons in Education) Journal*.

Teachers Planet: Technology

http://teachersplanet.com/tech.htm

From the Teachers Planet Web site, this is a brief listing of education technology resources from the U.S. Department of Education, NASA, the Computer Learning Foundation, and other sources. Although these sites are not necessarily for beginners, they are worth exploring and offer many practical resources.